FOR
CASOY RICE
GOOD LUCK

D1006611

WARREN MILLER

Lurching
from one near disaster to the next

Written and illustrated by the same guy.

Published by the Pole Pass Publishing Company. P.O. Box 350 Deer Harbor, Washington 98243.
Regarding personal appearance information, please use email: info@warrenmiller.net

The Pole Pass Publishing Company is a wholly owned subsidiary of the Lost Island Printing Company that is a subsidiary of the Ajax Mortgage Company.

Manufactured in the United States of America and in Seattle specifically from recycled trees.

Library of Congress Cataloging and Publication Data.

Some of the stories in this 1998 collection were originally published in the following: The Vail Daily, The Mammoth Times, The Summit Weekly, Ski Magazine, Snow Country, Reno Air Approach, Impact, Northwest Boating, Anacortes American, The Truckee Times, Aspen Daily, The Tahoe World, The Revue-Herald, the Inyo Register, the Tahoe Bonanza, City Sports Magazine, the Lone Peak Lookout, the Mountain Times, and the Mountaineer. They were also turned down by magazines and newspapers too numerous to mention.

Miller, Warren.

Warren Miller, LURCHING FROM ONE NEAR DISASTER TO THE NEXT/ 1st edition. Unfortunately the Library of Congress was too busy to return any of my letters of inquiry or my many phone calls. I did leave my name and phone number on 43 different voice-mail, tape recorders but apparently they all got erased. If you want further information, you can get it from the publishers or through the ISBN number.

ISBN: 0-9636144-2-8 (Soft Cover)
ISBN: 0-9636144-3-6 (Hard Cover)

First edition, 1998

Disclaimer: Some of the names and locations of the stories have been changed. I can sometimes remember where the event happened, but I have trouble remembering when and who it happened to. My apologies to you if the shoe fits and it hurts a little.

DEDICATION

In 1957, I wrote WINE, WOMEN, WARREN, AND SKIS, a book about living all winter in the parking lot at Sun Valley, Idaho, and I dedicated it to "Miss Abigail Nicelunchkowski, inventor of the oyster cracker. Without her foresight in offering vitamin-enriched oyster crackers to the Union Pacific Railroad for their Sun Valley, Idaho, operation, I might never have survived the cold winter of 1946/47. Good luck to you, Miss Abigail Nicelunchkowski, wherever you are."

Even back then, I was lurching dangerously from one near disaster to the next.

I would like to dedicate *this* book to the many people who have saved me from lurching too far, too often. For the time I ran out of gas in the middle of Colorado in a blizzard, I'd like to thank the farmer who stopped and sold me a gallon of gas for only ten dollars. I'd like to thank the banker who used to loan me money on the pink slip for my '56 Chevy so I could pay my bill at the film lab (and that was in 1964). I'd also like to thank the many people, known and unknown, who have taken me in tow when the wind dropped to zero and I was still a long way from the beach in my catamaran or on my windsurfer. Also, the many ski resort owners and managers who gave me free lift tickets, long before I was old enough to get one as a senior citizen.

I'd like to thank the cameramen who in recent years have taken all of those great ski pictures that I still, somehow, get the credit for. Thanks to the many people who have come to our ski movies and gone home, wisely quit their jobs, rented a U-haul trailer, and moved to a ski resort. Thanks to all of the newspaper editors who have published my weekly newspaper columns so I would have enough stories to publish another book. I want to thank YOU in particular for buying a copy of this book so I can stay **retired**, with my wife, Laurie, and keep on lurching from one near disaster to the next.

Thank you also to Maureen Dickson at Cap Sante Marine, for fixing all the stuff we break on the boat and for keeping us alive in our water adventures.

Probably the most important thank you goes to Barbara Dillman, my indefatigable editor who works hard and long, trying to make my ramblings understandable and keep me from making a complete fool of myself.

And finally, a thank you to that elusive hexagonal shape that assumes geometric differences in numbers beyond belief. It has been estimated that if all of the snowflake patterns that have fallen since snow was invented were laid end to end, they would still all melt by late April.

INTRODUCTION TO WARREN MILLER

Written by Hugo Guldenfinger

If you asked a hundred people to describe Warren Miller, you would get a completely different visual person out of each one of their descriptions.

Don Byers used to say, "Warren treats nickels like they were manhole covers."

Maybe he does, but since he grew up in the bottom of the depression in a very dysfunctional family, it takes a long time to change your ways when your first job was making ten cents a day in a grocery store, sorting eggs and sweeping floors.

Ted Nicholson says, "In high school in Hollywood, Warren was one of only five of us who owned a surfboard. This was before the invention of the wetsuit or fiberglass. His surfboard had a lot of redwood in it to keep it from getting dinged up. It also weighed almost a hundred pounds. "

With a little time out - three-and-a-half years to be exact - Warren helped with the World War Two efforts by going to college, getting a commission in the Navy, going overseas, and getting sunk in a hurricane.

After the war, having already owned a pair of skis for eight years, he bought two pair of army surplus, stiff, seven-foot-six-inch, white ones, scraped the paint off of them, varnished them, and sold one pair for $25. With $20, he bought army surplus poles, ski boots, a parka, a pair of goggles, a hat, a sweater, a pair of gloves, and a pair of pants.

Warren also bought his first motion picture camera, 8mm, and produced his first surfing epic at Malibu in 1946. That summer, he bought a small trailer and went skiing non-stop for the next two winters.

No one bothered to tell him that it would be cold sleeping in an eight-foot-long trailer without heat in the below-zero weather of ski resort parking lots. The manager of Sun Valley, Pat Rogers, let Warren and his partner, Ward Baker, live in the parking lot for two winters as local color. Warren skied every day, learned to race, and then became a ski instructor during the winter of 1948/49.

When the new resort of Squaw Valley, California, opened with one chairlift and two rope tows, Warren got a job teaching skiing there for $125 a month and room and board. At night, he drew cartoons and sold them to the guests to help make enough money to buy film for his new 16mm camera. He was able to produce his first feature-length, ski film on a total budget of $427.

For the next three years, Warren lived mostly in the back of a panel delivery truck and pounded nails as a carpenter, framing tract houses. He also managed to somehow produce a new feature-length ski movie each year on the money he took in by showing his previous effort. Concurrent to all this, he married and had his first child, a son. He watched his young wife die of cancer of the spine when their son was only eighteen months old. Scott has become a director of photography, with nine Cleos to his credit.

Four years later, Warren remarried and had two more children, daughter Chris, who is a still photographer, and son Kurt, who bought the feature ski-film business.

The endless traveling to film ski resorts, selling commercial movies, running a business with 16 employees, and appearing with his film live for almost a hundred nights every year brought an end to this marriage.

The ski club presidents who used to bring his ski movies to your town had to make the decision whether or not to have Warren come and narrate the film in person for $200. Or choose one of the other eight or ten feature ski film producers who were making the rounds in the 1950's and '60's.

Fortunately, a lot of the more successful ski clubs chose to promote Warren's work.

One year, Warren visited 106 cities and slept in over 200 different hotels. That spring someone said, "Warren, didn't you know that you could put your voice right on the movie?" He did that and was then able to almost give up traveling. Then in 1989, he sold his film company to his son and his partner.

Now all Warren has to do is write the script for their annual feature film, go to a sound studio and record it on the sound track, and then go salmon fishing.

A major turning point in Warren's life was when he was a skiing bachelor at the top of Mt. Baldy in Sun Valley, Idaho, drawing cartoons for a group of young children. A pretty brunette came over and apologized for her son hanging around.

Warren said,

"It's no problem. But I've met you before."

The brunette replied, "You probably say that to most of the people you meet and take a chance that they were in an auditorium somewhere watching one of your films. Right?"

"No" Warren said. "I've met you before. It was seven or eight years ago and I had a breakfast meeting with you and Mike Wiegele in the Edgewater Inn in Seattle. You gave me a business card with blue ink on it.

I can't remember what it said, but it had blue ink on it. Is that correct?"

It was.

When Warren asked her for her address and phone number she gave it to him. But, when he got back to his condo, he discovered that unfortunately she had given him her Seattle address and phone number.

The next morning Warren worked until about ten-thirty, leisurely drove over to the Warm Springs lift, and while standing in line, hollered,

"Single."

The pretty brunette, Laurie, skied up and they rode up on the lift together. A few runs later, Warren dug some trail mix out of one of his pockets and invited her to lunch. He had to blow the feathers out of it because he was wearing a ten-year-old, faded green, White Stag vest. The few feathers that were left in his down vest were stuck behind duct tape that was holding the rips and tears together.

Three years later, Warren married Laurie, the lady he had breakfasted with in the Edgewater Inn eleven years before.

Five years ago, while skiing with Gene Young, who was currently a vice-president of Bantam Books, Warren talked to her about writing his autobiography. He managed to talk her into reading a copy of his book, WINE, WOMEN, WARREN AND SKIS. After she read it, her comment was, "Warren, you are not a very good writer. If you want to write your autobiography, you better hire a ghostwriter.

He told her, "My brain is full of ghosts of the past. I need a new career about this time in my life so I guess it'll be writing. I can get my lift tickets free because I'm finally old enough; besides, what else is there to do when the powder snow is breakable crust?"

That was six years ago. Now Warren is officially retired, sort of, and writing a newspaper column for a dozen weekly newspapers, while trying to learn how to catch salmon. He's also learning (out of self-preservation) how to repair a 44-foot sport fisherman with two Cummins 400 horsepower engines, a water maker, a bathtub, dishwasher, and washing machine and dryer (because things can be get wet while on a boat), and a generator, so that he and Laurie can have a nice place to live while cruising to Alaska. He is also trying to ski a hundred or more days a year, break 115 for a round of golf, and catch the wily salmon in his lair, as he still continues to lurch from one near disaster to the next.

"Lurching is good for you, if you keep it in perspective", he says.

Eight months a year Warren does most of his lurching while living on a small island near the Canadian border. The other four months of Warren's lurching time is spent cruising around the ski resorts of the world.

Look for Warren's trailer in the parking lot where you ski next winter. It's a big white one with four wheels; Warren and Laurie will be somewhere near the ski lift selling and autographing copies of this book as a fund raiser for whatever is the charity of their choice, that week, at that ski resort.

CONTENTS

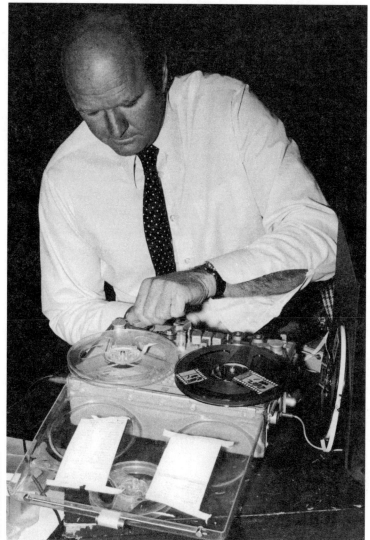

*"For almost forty years I would unpack
my tape recorder, set up my projector
and film, and tell my stories against a
background of music and color film."*

THE STORYTELLER

The other day in Sullivan Bay, Canada, after I lost another salmon, my fishing guide said, "What was it you used to do for a living?"

"I've always been a storyteller," I replied

"I hope you're not like that guy in Boston, what's his name, Mike Barnicle, who got busted for stealing George Carlin's jokes and putting them in his newspaper column."

I thought about that for a minute and said, "If I had been born two hundred years ago, I would have been the guy who traveled from town to town telling stories about the people who lived in the town I had just left."

I am doing that today, and, if repeating a story someone told me a day, a week, or a month ago is stealing his or her story, then so be it. However, I have been telling stories with film and music for the last fifty years and I have about a million stories, give or take a few. These are stories that I have been told, that I read about in some small-town newspaper, or experienced myself that have never been told in any of the hundreds of movies I have made.

If I repeat a story that someone else told me twenty years ago, is it stealing a story? Someone once told me, "There is no such thing as an original story. Everyone just copies from someone else, alters it a little, and conceals the source of the original story."

What if I told the story about driving our boat full speed through a place called Hole-in-the-Wall, where the current runs over eight knots at full flood? We were dodging whirlpools and feeling our 30,000-pound, 44-foot-long boat being thrown around like a feather in a gust of wind. In the middle of negotiating the rapids, I saw two logs heading my way and forcing me dangerously close to the rocks on my left. I have read a lot about people up in British Columbia experiencing the same rapids who didn't survive.

Is it stealing a story to write about a man who grew up on Saltspring Island around the turn of the century where, as a teenager, his uncle showed up one day from Tennessee? The uncle had walked from Tennessee to Vancouver, British Columbia, pushing all of his belongings in a wheelbarrow with a metal wheel. But the road out was a dirt road, so his hands could handle it.

I have written about my wife and myself getting sucked backwards into a whirlpool where, if the transom of our boat had not been as high above the water as it was, we would have sunk without a trace in about a minute or less.

I have read stories of a ship over 100 feet long, with 50 passengers onboard, spinning in a giant whirlpool until it started sinking, completely revolving a dozen times, as it slowly got sucked under water like a spider in a bathroom sink, until only the top half of the masts could be seen. They were still spinning when they too got sucked under and disappeared, without so much as a single piece of the vessel or a body ever washing ashore.

It is exciting to sit on the dock and hear some of these old-time stories, and it is exciting to ride on a ski lift and be an old timer and tell some of my own old-time experiences.

Is it stealing a story to write about Sun Valley, Idaho, when they had only four single chairlifts operating and slept 843 people, with 843 employees, and vacant lots in nearby Ketchum, selling for $350? I know it is true because I bought my first piece of real estate for that amount of money

Back in 1952, I started printing a small program to give away at my ski movie showings. In the editorial portion, I wrote about living in the parking lot in Sun Valley all winter while skiing every day and only spending $18. I had room at the end of that story for another paragraph and the printer said, "Why don't you call your story, EXCERPTS FROM MY FORTHCOMING BOOK."

I did, but I added another sentence, "To reserve your copy at the pre-publication discount price of $2, mail me a postcard and I will send you a copy C.O.D. when it is published." Over a thousand people sent me $2. The next winter, the headline for the story in my movie program was GOOD GRIEF, MORE EXCERPTS, and people started writing me for their $2 back. I had already spent the money, so I had to write and publish another book. WINE, WOMEN, WARREN, AND SKIS was the result.

It is obvious that I am a storyteller at heart, an observer of human nature with a wry sense of humor. Sometimes I wonder if my lurching from one near-disaster to another is due to the fact that I am always out there looking for the next story, instead of watching what I am doing and where I am going in life. But, it's been a great life, a story worth telling.

*"I'm a fourteen year old kid trapped
in a senior citizen's body."*

THE PARTY

I've spent most of my life lurching from one near-disaster to the next and writing about them. One week, for the first time in my memory, there were no disasters: instead, there was a weekend-long birthday party that I'd like to share with you.

Somehow, through months of devious planning and secrecy on the part of a lot of people, 162 of my friends managed to find their way to this small island in the Northwest. They came to have a seafood dinner, a boat ride to Victoria, another seafood dinner at a port on the way back, and spend two or three nights in a strange cabin somewhere, all because seventy years ago Warren Miller started going downhill.

Yep, it was the Big Seven Oh!

I could write a book about what my wife must have gone through to coordinate my surprise party without me ever finding out about it. What I wonder now is, what else has she been doing since we found each other that I don't know about?

My publisher and I had lunch a week or so ago and he told me that there were a lot of mix-ups on the press schedule so, consequently, my new book would be delayed a couple of weeks. I now realize that was all a smoke screen because, during his speech at the party, he produced the first 165 copies of the book, WARREN MILLER, ON FILM, IN PRINT, one for each of the guests who had traveled so far. So in addition to it being my BIG SEVEN OH, it was also the introductory party for my new book.

5

It's a collection of some of the articles that have appeared in THE VAIL DAILY and a lot that have not, stories of Warren as he lurches through life from one near-disaster to the next.

But Laurie's surprise party was anything but a near-disaster. First, there was a quiet dinner on Friday night with two of my three children and my sister. The next day, we took a boat ride and had a hamburger barbecue in the afternoon. Then, under the guise of showing my family what our property looked like from the water, we were sitting just off-shore on my next door neighbor, Hobie Alter's big catamaran, when out of our house and garden, 162 people appeared in matching white T-shirts to sing Happy Birthday. They looked (but didn't sound like) the Mormon Tabernacle Choir as they sang.

If any of them had been carrying crosses, I would really have been worried.

This was followed by a couple of hours of, "Haven't seen you for years," and "You haven't changed a bit," cocktail-party exchanges and then everyone disappeared, only to reappear at a lodge dining room a mile or so away that was built in 1927. There, the 162 people had a sit-down, salmon dinner and I got to listen to a couple of hours of being roasted.

John Sununu started it off with,

"I just traveled 3,500 miles. I rode on two different airlines, had a two-hour drive in a rental car, an hour-and-a-half ferryboat ride and another half-hour drive to get here. I don't know where I am. How in the devil did Warren end up here?"

Slim Sommerville stood up and said, "Lewis and Clark would never have been able to make it here on their own. But they had Sackajawea. Warren made it here only because he has Sacka-Laurie." And, with that, the party officially got underway.

6

I was overwhelmed, feeling so lucky to have so many wonderful friends.

Sunday morning we all met at the dock for a boat ride to Victoria, B.C, lunch at Butchart Gardens, and then a boat ride back to Roche Harbor for another great dinner party. At that party, Dick Hauserman said, "We have tried to get a mountain named after Warren, but the red tape stopped us. However, we have been able to get a street in Vail named after him. In the future, Warren, when you are skiing at Vail, you can look down into the valley and point to yourself and say proudly, I-70."

At that party, Jack Smith, Dr. Richard Hawkins, and Jack Kemp said some nice things about Laurie's and my involvement in both the Steadman/Hawkins Foundation in Vail and Dave McCoy's Foundation in Mammoth to build a college.

The fact that I have managed to survive to the age of 70, was easily overshadowed by the incredible planning and complete secrecy with which my wife carried off the weekend without my knowing anything about it. One hundred and sixty-two people are a substantial number to arrange rooms for on a small island with very limited accommodations; ferryboat rides, airplane rides, and tie-downs at the local airport. Yes, it was wonderful to be able to combine it with the introduction of my new book and send everyone home with their own copy, as well as a head and heart full of good memories.

Many of the people had never met before, but by Sunday evening they had a common denominator of complete exhaustion and a host of newfound best friends.

Two of the couples were so taken by the location and the scenery that they didn't go on the

Sunday boat ride to Victoria. Instead, they hired real estate agents and started looking at property.

The only thing I missed at the party was that my son Scott couldn't make it, because he was in the middle of directing a big-budget television commercial.

Laurie won't tell me how much the party cost, but I do know that I am going to have to sell a lot of copies of this book before we are out of the red on my Book Introduction/Seventieth Birthday Party.

In the meantime, I know that I'll keep on lurching through some new disasters in order to have the material to keep on writing stories.

IN SEARCH OF FREEDOM

It doesn't take a very long sentence to completely alter one's life.

Over the years, there have been half a dozen or so short sentences that completely changed my life. In 1933, at the bottom of the depression, I was the only kid in my fourth grade class who had a job. I was earning ten cents every Saturday for spending all day in the neighborhood grocery store. I swept the floor, carried fresh produce, stacked groceries, and made myself indispensable to the owner because of what he said to me. "As long as you come to work on time and work hard, you can have a job here."

In October of that same year, when I turned nine, my grandmother said, "Warren, here are a pair of roller skates for your birthday."

The next morning, I was out of bed by 4:30, trying to learn how to roller-skate.

Those roller skates gave me my first experience with a commodity called freedom. That eleven-word sentence my grandmother spoke, and her gift, changed my life forever.

Since then, other short sentences, or questions, have also dramatically changed my life.

At the age of thirteen, my woodshop teacher in the eighth grade said, "Warren, I have a set of plans for a surfboard that I cut out of Popular Mechanics. Would you like to try to build one?" The surfboard was five feet long and two feet wide, box-square, hollow, and leaked a lot. Whenever I could get anyone to haul it, and me, to the beach, I was finding more freedom.

That same year, 1937, when our Boy Scout troop came home from a long weekend trip to the snow in the local San Bernardino Mountains, I somehow crossed paths with someone who had a pair of skis for sale that were hanging in his garage in downtown Hollywood. The $2 that I spent for the skis and poles turned out to be the most important $2 that I ever spent in my life. They were made out of pine, had no edges, and had leather toe straps for bindings. Just like that first pair of roller skates, I now had a freedom vehicle strapped to my feet and could go wherever there was snow. All I had to do was learn how to use them, which I'm still trying to do 61 years later!

By the time I was fifteen years old, a high school friend named Ted Nicholson said, "I'm going to San Onofre this weekend to go surfing. If you have a sleeping bag and can round up a loaf of bread and a jar of peanut butter, you're welcome to come along in the rumble seat." That weekend, when he was too tired to surf anymore, he let me use his genuine Hawaiian surfboard. It was so big and heavy I couldn't lift it. It weighed one hundred pounds, so I had to drag it across the beach. I somehow managed to paddle out to where the waves were at least two feet high. Nearing exhaustion, I was barely able to paddle hard enough, catch a small wave that had already broken, and somehow stand up.

That one invitation to San Onofre was another sentence that changed my life forever by offering me even more freedom.

Over the course of my life, my search for freedom has dictated almost everything I have ever pursued. For the next twenty years, I surfed all summer

10

and skied all winter (even during most of my three-and-a-half-year stint in the Navy). Sure, I took a little time out here and there to run a camera and try to explain to the people who came to see my ski movies that my philosophy was different than most people's. By the time I was 35 years old, I knew that a very simple gift or the right sentence could alter anyone's life. It could send them in search of their own individual freedom.

I believe that in every city the streets are straight, the buildings and rooms in them are square, and our bodies are sort of round, so they don't belong inside the buildings in the cities.

In 1962, someone said, "I have a great sailing catamaran I think you would enjoy. Can I give you a ride?"

Within two hundred yards of when we sailed away from the dock, I knew I was going to buy that catamaran. And so, for the next twenty years, I sailed and raced a variety of boats every chance I had. And, often, I sailed or raced boats when I shouldn't have.

One day in the late 1960's, at a sailboat regatta, Hoyle Schweitzer said, "I've invented this thing I call a windsurfer. I would like you to try it."

When I got on that windsurfer #38, it had a mind of its own, just like that first pair of skis had a mind of their own. That same windsurfer took me wherever it wanted to.

Today, I have a quiver of sails, four windsurfers, and the perfect condo to sail from in Maui, but several years ago, my wife Laurie showed me pictures of Glacier Bay, Alaska. Giant blocks of ice hundreds of feet tall tumbling into the frigid ocean with a thirty-foot boat rocking and rolling from the waves that the tumbling glacier kicked up. That

11

glacier is nine hundred miles by boat from where we live in the summer, up near the Canadian border. When my wife showed me the pictures of Glacier Bay she said, "Warren, thousands of people have made the trip to Glacier Bay in small boats during your lifetime. If you don't do it this year, you'll be one year older when you do."

I now have our windsurfing condo for sale in Maui.

I'm glad I passed on trying to learn how to snowboard last winter.

Over a hundred years ago some prospectors came back from Alaska with a ton of gold. I know I'll come back from Alaska this summer with memories that will be worth at least ninety-seven and a half tons of gold and there is always next winter to try to learn how to snowboard. Ah, freedom!

OVERNIGHT SUCCESS

There were good days and there were bad days but, for decades, I traveled over l00,000 miles a year with two cans of film under my arm, a tape recorder, and a suitcase full of dirty laundry. I did as many as 106 live, narrated performances of my then current ski film during any one fall and winter season. I did those shows in as many as 106 different theaters, bars, and restaurants, in as many as 106 different cities. That same fiscal year, I slept in 212 different hotels and motels.

And, for those four decades, the routine was pretty much the same.

I would always get a wake-up call at about 5:30 a.m. in what was equivalent to a $6 or $7 motel, grab a taxi to the airport or walk to the bus depot, or drive my car to the next town for the next show. Sometimes the trip between the shows would be an hour or two, sometimes clear across America, from Seattle to Boston on a midnight plane after the show. But it would almost always be seven shows in seven cities in seven days, from the middle of October until just before Christmas. Then, I would again show the film all through January, the first two weeks of February, and then start traveling to film the next year's movie.

I always tried to arrive at the theater at least an hour before show time to make sure that the promoter had the right projector, screen, and sound system. More often than not, one or more of the three components necessary for the show would be either broken or missing. So, in addition to my own tape

13

deck and film, I always carried about five pounds of tools and spare parts. That way, I could usually jury-rig my way out of most any problem.

The first thing I would do when I arrived was to renew my acquaintance with the janitor or the stage manager, depending on the size of the auditorium. Then I would haul out some rickety old table that I had hidden somewhere backstage the year before, set up my tape recorder, and check sound levels. The next stop would be the long climb up to the projection booth. There I would clean the gate on the projector because in many cases the projector had not been cleaned since the year before when I had done it.

The audience was different every night, both in attitude and attendance.

Such as one night in Pennsylvania.

I knew I was in trouble when the promoter invited me to have dinner with him at 7 p.m. when the show started at 8 p.m. The show was going to be held in a suburban high school auditorium so I said,

"I'll pass on dinner so I can get everything checked out before the show."

Olaf replied,

"If you know where the school is, then I will meet you there after I eat dinner."

I knew I was in very serious trouble when I arrived at the school because the theater was dark, so I sat in my rented car until 7:15, when the janitor finally showed up to let me in. It was a real scramble for me to get all of the equipment in order for the 8:00 performance. I was the only person in the auditorium except the janitor. However, I didn't worry too much because this time I had a guarantee of $175 for the evening, $25 more than my usual fee back in 1955. I would be okay but I didn't know about the show.

14

I had everything set up by 7:45, when the promoter showed up with what was left of his six-pack dinner. He quickly sold eight tickets for $1.50 each to the eight people who had been waiting in line.

That was it!

Eight people paid admission to fill up a 1300-seat auditorium. I wandered out into the parking lot to see if we should hold the show up in case of any late arrivals.

There were none.

I was chatting with the policeman out front who was hired to handle the anticipated crowd, when an elderly lady strolled out of the darkness. She was the geometry teacher at the high school and lived nearby. She had been out walking her dog and saw the lights on at the school so decided to come by to see what was going on.

As I went back inside to get the show started, I invited both the policeman and the geometry teacher, with her dog, to come in and see the show.

I wandered around the theater and introduced myself to the other eight people who had paid their $1.50 to see my latest ski film, featuring Stein Erickson, Christian Pravda, Dick Buek and 8 year-old, Jimmy Heuga. Then I invited them to all sit down front, where we could all share the ski experience closer together.

I then climbed up on the stage and talked to the 1290 empty seats and the ten full ones as though the auditorium was completely full. That, of course, didn't include the geometry teacher's dog. I told a few stories about the film and where it was going to take them and then asked to janitor to turn out the lights and the 13 year-old projectionist to turn on the projector.

When the house lights went out, the projection room electricity went off, too. So in the few minutes of total darkness in the building, I chatted some more with the ten people in the audience. Eleven, if you count the promoter who was popping the lid on the last remaining bottle in his six-pack.

While the lights were being figured out by the janitor, I thought about the good advice I had been given the year I showed my first ski film, in 1950.

That time, there were 37 people in the Sun Valley Opera House, a theater that normally seats about 300. The old-timer who was running the theater had been a vaudeville performer, and he gave me the advice that would see me through a lot of the ups and downs of show business. I still think about that advice almost fifty years later:

1. Always entertain the people who show up, and feel sorry for the people who don't.

2. You are going to work all your life to become an overnight success.

3. Never stop working at it.

I have applied that same advice to this book that you have just bought. Whether 15 people or 1500 people read it, I have given it my best. I am still hoping to become an overnight success!

*"You are going to have to work all
of your life to be a success overnight."*

"I remember that I was just phasing out of my Boy Scout career in favor of girls, when I saw this picture of Dick Durrance in a sporting goods store in downtown Los Angeles. This was not long after someone invented the rope tow and a year or two after they invented Sun Valley, Idaho, and the chair lift. Seeing that photograph changed my life forever."

SKI RACING AND TREE REMOVAL

In 1939, a narrow, dusty, dirt road led northwest from the small, almost-abandoned mining town of Ketchum, Idaho. About two miles in that same direction, an even narrower, winding ski trail that had been cut the summer before, led from the top of 9,000-foot high, Mt. Baldy. Just upstream from this point, where the trail met the valley floor, hot sulfur springs flow into the Big Wood River. Here and there was a natural pool you could soak your tired body in, even during the below-zero days of January.

On the eastern side of Mt. Baldy and about three or four miles downstream from the Hot Springs, one of the first chairlifts ever built in the world carried skiers across its steaming waters. The River Run chairlift was the first of three that could carry over 400 people an hour, 3,000 vertical feet to the top of Baldy, in a little less than half an hour.

Skiing was coming of age in America while the ravages of war were beginning to race across Europe.

A young man named Dick Durrance from Florida, by way of Germany and an eighth-place finish in the 1936 Olympics, was the pre-race favorite to win the first downhill race ever held from the top of Baldy. The downhill race was named after the visionary who founded Sun Valley, Idaho, Averill Harriman. This downhill race would prove to be the toughest that America had to offer.

Partway down the winding, narrow trail, there was an awesome steilhung that faced due south. At

19

the bottom, it a had a wicked transition and left turn that could give any skier with enough courage more speed than his equipment or his body could handle.

I'm talking about stiff, wooden, ridge-top, hickory, 7' 6" skis without p-tex bottoms or offset edges, and bindings that would not release in any direction, no matter how you fell. With skis that long, often, when you fell, your body would sometimes revolve a time or two more than your legs would.

Halfway down Warm Springs, the downhill race trail designer, Friedl Pfeiffer, had cut seven turns that were very narrow and twisting because the hill was so steep. Each one required a rather abrupt turn to miss the trees on either side, turns that the better racers tried to straighten out as much as possible so they could go faster. As they did, they alternately came dangerously close to the trees on either side of the trail.

Dick Durrance, with all the skill born of nearly a dozen years of ski racing experience, kept looking and looking for a faster line through these seven dangerous turns.

The race course committee felt that the trees were so close together that they would become the control gates, so no artificial control gates were necessary in this part of the course. There simply was no straight line through the seven turns for a shortcut.

Dick spent a lot of time in this part of the course, sighting through the trees, looking at them every which way, until he finally had it figured out.

If one tree in particular was cut down, he could straighten out all seven turns and save an enormous amount of time.

Why not?

Late in the afternoon on the day before the race, Dick climbed up Warm Springs with a saw, a shovel, and a friend; together, they sawed down that one tree that stood in the way of Dick's secret short-cut. Not a large tree but, nevertheless, one that was definitely in the way of that straight line that bypassed the seven turns that he wanted to avoid.

Once they dragged the tree out of the way, they returned to cover the scattered pine needles that had fallen with the new snow.

Now all that remained for Dick to do was climb back up the course and decide where he could get lined up for his straight shot through the seven turns. Once that was determined, he decided not to ski the line at that time because someone else might see his tracks and try it too.

Now that the racing line was figured out, they found another smaller tree, sawed it down, and carried it gently over to where the first tree had been cut down. There, they propped it upright in the same place as the original tree.

After half a dozen rehearsals of quick-tree removal by Dick's partner, their plan was all set.

As soon as it was determined which racing number Dick would have, his partner would simply count the racers as they went by and then yank the substitute tree out of the way so Dick could take his shortcut. He wouldn't have to make all seven turns. Once Dick raced by, his partner would reinsert the tree so no one else could go as straight.

Everything worked perfectly, as racers #1 through #3 roared by, making their much slower and wider turns around all seven angles in this part of the course.

"O.K. yank out the tree! NOW!"

Dick roared through on his one-of-a-kind straight line and the substitute tree was immediately reinserted, as he sped on down the course in complete control.

Dick forgot one thing, however. He roared out of that section without turns, at such a high rate of speed that he missed the final turn at the bottom of the course – a right turn to the finish line.

Instead, he skidded on and on until he wound up splashing around, knee-deep in the Big Wood River. While using up precious time, he somehow managed to clamber up out of the ice-cold water, climb on up to the finish line, and fall across it to win the race by two full seconds.

Dick was the first winner of the Harriman Cup. For all of his foresight and skill, he still had to ride back to the Lodge in his wet ski boots and clothes.

Three days later, Dick was fined $2 by the Forest Service for chopping down a tree on government property without a permit.

"I think the truck Dick Durrance drove home from the Harriman Cup in 1939 is the same one I drove to Seattle to pick up my rowboat in 1997."

THE TRUCK FROM HELL

I took a few days off from skiing and flew up to the Seattle Boat Show to check out all of the new fifty-foot powerboats and also to see if my new rowboat was finished yet.

The rowboat was finished, but it was down in Gig Harbor, about a hundred and twenty miles from our home in the San Juan Islands.

Rather than row it all the way home, I borrowed a pickup truck from my friend Elmo, who has a local gardening business here on the island. He raises grass. Anyone with the name of Elmo can only drive a pickup truck. Fortunately for me, he was away on his annual vacation with his camera, filming wild animals on the Serengeti.

His wife Abigail said, "It is O.K. to use the truck but, be very careful of it."

The odometer only had 34,000 miles on it but, before I had gotten halfway to the ferry dock, I realized that this was the third or fourth hundred-thousand-mile round-rip on Elmo's odometer. The steering wheel was a souvenir from Elmo's eighteen-wheeler-driving days and about three feet in diameter. The steering was a little loose, so it took about three-eighths of a revolution before anything would happen to the front wheels.

I had my first real problem with the truck on the way to the ferry when I had a flat tire. Elmo's spare tire was one of those little bitsy things that they always have hidden in the trunk of a compact rental car. I limped the rest of the way to the ferry at about twenty miles an hour with the left front end of the truck about twenty inches higher than the right.

When I got off the ferry at Anacortes, I was heading for the tire shop to buy Elmo a new tire in exchange for loaning me the truck, when the truck died. Despite what the gas gauge said, I was out of gas.

I was luckier with this disaster because I coasted into the gas station and filled up both of Elmo's gas tanks for $53.47. After I paid the bill, I noticed that Elmo's wife had left a note on the seat of the truck that said that I should only use 96 octane, expensive gasoline, and not to fill up the front tank because it leaked and dribbled into the cab of the truck.

By the time I had bought the new tire and was again on the road to pick up my rowboat, eleven gallons of the gas in the front tank had flowed across the floor of the cab and out a hole in the floor by the throttle. I stopped and bought a big Mack and four orders of fries and squashed the fries all over the floor of the truck to soak up the gasoline smell. Potatoes always work!

I was already one hour late, but I was finally headed down I-5 to pick up my toy.

The ferry charges an extra $28 if your truck is too tall so, in order to save money, I just slid my new rowboat into the bed of the truck like a pile of lumber, instead of putting it on top of the lumber rack above the cab. Twenty-eight dollars saved is twenty-eight dollars saved.

I paid the bill for the boat, lashed it down tightly, and started back north. The weather changed from sun to rain, to hail, to snow, to sun. Naturally, it was raining the hardest when I had to stop at the Kingdome where the Boat Show was being held, to pick up the second set of oarlocks for our new boat.

Since the rowboat stuck six feet out of the back of Elmo's pickup truck, they charged me the motor-home rate to park the truck, $12, and sent me off into the far end of the parking lot.

It was then that I discovered that the key to Elmo's ignition didn't work in the door of the truck so I couldn't lock it up. Now I had to take my rucksack with me that contained my address book, my camera and two lenses, nine rolls of film, my parka, my dark glasses, my cellular phone, and two fishing reels that I had had repaired and picked up on the way to Gig Harbor.

The rowboat maker's wife was nice enough to loan me a free pass to pick up the oarlocks, but the pass didn't work on the side of the Kingdome I was parked on. Now, I had to walk about a million blocks to the other side of a 40,000-seat stadium to get in free.

I located my rowboat builder's booth and picked up my two oarlocks. My rucksack was now really full of stuff. When I tried to leave the building, the guard wouldn't let me out because I didn't have a receipt for the pair of oarlocks or my two recently repaired fishing reels.

I was treated as though I had just been caught trying to sneak a Smith-and-Wesson, 38-caliber revolver through the x-ray machine at airport security.

Fifty-three minutes later, the equivalent of the Kingdome Gestapo released me on my own recognizance and I began to slowly inch my way through the departing Boat Show traffic into the rush-hour commuter stream of traffic. It was precisely then that the truck coughed to a stop. I was once again out of gas. This time I knew enough to try to turn the switch to the other tank of gas. There was just enough left in it to get me to a gas station. There, I once again filled the back gas tank and spent half an hour replacing all of the fuses in the truck so the headlights wouldn't go off and on in rhythm to the windshield wipers. I also calculated that Elmo's truck got 6.7 miles per gallon.

At about 6pm, I finally merged into the commuter traffic headed north on I-5 from downtown Seattle. Swerving erratically back and forth between the two outside lanes with the loose steering mechanism on Elmo's truck, I rather enjoyed the leisurely drive back to Anacortes. Except for the two times the highway patrol stopped me! The first time was for drunk driving, but I passed the breatholator-walk-the-line-test. The second time was because the red flag on my boat wasn't big enough and the rowboat stuck out the back of the truck nineteen inches more than was allowed by law.

An hour later, I still had forty-five minutes to wait in the ferry line, so I stopped for my usual in-route-dinner of good old Colonel Sanders chicken, cholesterol, and lemonade.

The ferry ride was uneventful, except that I was up near the bow of the boat and the wind was blowing about forty-five-mph. About every fourth, eight-foot wave broke over the car deck and splashed over the roof of the truck. I was kind of hoping the waves would come up over the floor and wash the gasoline smell out of the cab so I could take a nap without worrying about dying from the fumes.

I drove off the ferry about 10pm, almost twelve hours after I had driven on it in the morning. Then, I had a twenty-minute drive to get to our end of the island.

I came around Six Dead Cat corner a little too fast, heard a clunk, and watched my brand new rowboat slide past the truck and me and disappear into the bushes. The driving rain had once again turned to sleet, so the boat actually slid on the ice, dirt, and asphalt, as smooth as if it was in the water. My Boy Scout knots didn't hold as well as I had thought they would. Fortunately, one piece of rope was long enough so I could attach it to the boat way out in the bushes and tow it back to where I could wrestle it back onto the truck. I tried to tie better knots this time, even though the rope was frozen stiff.

Ten minutes later, I was mentally rowing the boat and never did see the deer that ran in front of the truck to commit suicide on my bumper and radiator.

I always carry a good, sharp, fish-cleaning knife in my rucksack, along with my camera, so I cut away that truck-bumper-hood-ornament-dead-deer and arrived home a bit later. I walked in the front door, to find my wife asleep on the couch in front of the television set. I was standing right over her, but didn't realize I was covered with deer blood and hair. She woke up when I said, "Surprise honey! Guess what happened?"

I still can't understand why she didn't appreciate my safe arrival with our new rowboat.

In the mid 1930's a young man walked into a bank in Bishop, California, and tried to borrow $84.00 on his motorcycle to buy the parts for a rope tow. That man is Dave McCoy. Today, he is the proud owner of a volcano called Mammoth Mountain, with 28 chairlifts and 2 gondolas.

WHERE HAVE ALL OF THE ENTREPRENEURS GONE?

In 1936, Averill Harriman created Sun Valley, Idaho, because he enjoyed skiing in St. Anton, Austria, before he became the president of the Union Pacific Railroad. His engineers invented the chair lift in the railroad yard in Omaha, Nebraska, in July. The parts were fabricated and transported to a remote hill near the end of the railroad in Ketchum, Idaho, hauled up the hill on the backs of mules, and the ski lift was running five months later, in time for Christmas.

In the 1930's, permits could be had for the asking and the American destination ski resort was invented.

That same year, a young man walked into a bank in Bishop, California, and tried to borrow $84 against his motorcycle to buy the parts for a rope tow. The banker turned him down and when he left, the banker's secretary said, "If you don't loan that nice young man that $84, I'm going to quit." The banker loaned Dave McCoy, the entrepreneur, the money to buy his first lift and since then he has built and owns all thirty-one of the lifts that are on Mammoth Mountain. At one time in his career, he even owned the bank that loaned him the $84. He married that banker's secretary, Roma, now a half-century ago.

In 1948, Sun Valley decided to build a new lift on Dollar Mountain. The manager of Sun Valley, Pappy Rogers, wanted $5,000 for the original single chair. Everett Kercher, an automobile salesman from Michigan, offered him $4,800 and bought the lift as is, where is. Everett and his ski school director, Victor Gotschalk, then took the lift apart, bolt by bolt, trucked it to nearby Ketchum where they loaded it on a train, and shipped it to Michigan. There, Everett made it into a double chairlift and put it up on the then four hundred-foot high Boyne Mountain. As the story goes, Boyne was a mountain Everett Kercher had purchased for less than $100 from a farmer because no crops could be grown on it. Today, the Kercher family owns Boyne Mountain, Boyne Highlands, Gatlinburgh, West Virginia, Big Sky, Montana, Crystal Mountain, Washington, and Solitude, Utah.

In the late 1930's, Wayne Poulsen and Marty Arroge bought a meadow in the Sierras for a rumored $10,000. In 1948, they sold part of it to Alex Cushing so he could build a chairlift.

Alex not only built a chairlift, he built two rope tows and I had the good fortune to teach skiing at Squaw Valley that first winter of 1949. On a good day, all four of us instructors would have a pupil. When the powder was too deep to teach, I took movies of the other instructors and the ski patrolmen, and produced my first feature-length ski film for less than $500.

In the mid 1950's, Jack Murphy who had been a bartender in Sun Valley, Idaho, got together with Damon Gad who was looking for a better place to ski in Vermont and together they created Sugarbush.

In the early 1960's, I got a phone call from the Treasurer of the Carnation Milk Company in Los Angeles. He wanted me to take some movies of a section of land he owned near Lake Tahoe. I flew up and spent the weekend in a helicopter with four or five skiers and put a promotional film together for John Riley. He took it out on the road and sold enough stock to build Alpine Meadows.

About that same time, Bob Mickelsen found an isolated quarter section of land within fifty miles of Seattle and a short distance from a six-lane freeway. I spent two days flying around in a helicopter with Jim Whittaker and three or four other skiers and put together a promotional film for Bob to sell vacant lots at his potential ski resort. The first morning he showed the film in Seattle, he sold seventy-one lots at what became Alpental.

In the late 1950's, a veteran of the Army Ski Troops found the place to build his ski resort. He built a scale model of his dream, put it in the back of his station wagon alongside his bed, and traveled all over America trying to interest people in buying vacant lots. He and some friends had bought a ranch under the guise of forming a Rod and Gun club. Those vacant lots sold for five and ten thousand dollars and you got a couple of lifetime lift-passes with them. The $20,000 houses that were built on those $5,000 lots in the 1960's have sold for as much as five million dollars in recent years. Pete Seibert, was the entrepreneur who created Vail, Colorado.

Throughout the fifties, sixties, and into the early seventies, destination ski resorts were being created at the rate of about one every year or two. Then, gradually, environmental concerns made the permit process impossible to cope with.

The last destination resort built in America was Deer Valley and that was in 1972, on private property. One man in California has invested seven million dollars of his own money and eight years of his life, trying to get a ski resort started near Mammoth. He is again shut down because someone

31

discovered a rare breed of fish that lives in the creek that runs through the valley at the bottom of his hill.

The current entrepreneurial spirit is to simply buy up existing resorts and homogenize them under one ownership. They are moving numbers around on a financial balance sheet and selling stock, instead of logging skiing trails, moving dirt, and building ski lifts.

It has been a fascinating fifty-year filming career to watch the change. I used to be able to phone someone and ask if I could stop by and take movies of their new resort. Boy, has that changed!

Last fall, I was looking for new things in the ski business. I telephoned a major ski resort for their 218-page color brochure. The electronic voice that answered said "S-p-e-l-l—y-o-u-r—n-a-m-e—a-n-d—a-d-d-r-e-s-s—s-l-o-w-l-y."

The space-age voice repeated the correct name and address and then said, "P-l-e-a-s-e—-a-l-l-o-w—-f-o-u-r—-t-o—-s-i-x—-w-e-e-k-s—-f-o-r—-d-e-l-i-v-e-r-y."

I made that phone call in November. Why would anyone wait six weeks for a travel brochure to plan a ski vacation? That same person can order eleven different items from The Land's End catalog and the garments will be delivered within forty-eight hours.

People go skiing for the pure gut feeling of turning a pair of skis on the side of a mountain. They go skiing where they can actually talk to a real person and get up-to-date information. What about men like Ted Johnson who was flipping hamburgers at the top of the lift at Alta? At the end of the day, he would ski over the ridge and down into the next valley. Before long, he was buying up old mining claims from little old ladies who lived in house trailers in

Torrance, California, and Minneapolis, Minnesota. When he had all of the mining claims and surface rights bought up, he raised the money and created Snowbird, Utah.

Where have all of the entrepreneur's gone? What would you be doing in the winter if they had not created your favorite ski resorts? You had better hope that this country doesn't make it any more difficult for entrepreneurs to venture out and create the things that make our lives more pleasurable.

In 1949 when Squaw Valley, California, opened with one chair lift and two rope tows, there were five ski instructors. From left to right: Dodie Post, Ski School director Emile Allais, Warren, Charlie Cole, and Alfred Hauser. On a busy day, we would all have at least one pupil.

"With the tide running against me, it was time to get out the emergency outboard motor."

OPENING DAY OF BOATING SEASON

Opening day of boating season can vary, depending on the type of boat you own. For years, while I raced high performance catamarans, I would sit in the boat storage area at the yacht club and watch while all of the blue-blazered officers gave their self-promotional speeches. Finally, some retired Navy or Coast Guard officer would tell the formally dressed members, "For safe boating, never leave the dock without wearing your life jackets." Then some half-drunk, retiring flag officer would pull the lanyard and the homemade cannon would blast off. Every opening day, some woman with the same shel-lacked, beehive-bouffant hairdo would squeal in fear at the cannon's explosion.

Up where we live in the Northwest, my open-ing day of boating is different and almost always challenging.

Yesterday was my opening day. I drove my 1976, twenty-foot powerboat (we call it a floating pickup truck) down to Anacortes for its annual power-wash-the-moss-off-its-bottom day.

Joe, our handyman who takes care of our island home in our absence, told me he had been having trouble with the boat engine not running at the proper rpm and to budget a little extra time to get wherever I was going.

The normal trip to Anacortes is forty-five min-utes to an hour, depending on the tidal current and how choppy the water is. My opening day journey took four-and-a-half hours.

The engine started easily and I let it warm up while I untied the dock lines and then eased away from the dock. Pulling the fenders aboard, I idled for the first 400 yards to get out of the no-wake zone of Pole Pass, and then I shoved the throttle forward and began running at 3200 rpm. That engine speed gives me about 25mph, which is fairly comfortable because I am very busy looking for floating logs and other debris that I don't want to hit.

One hundred yards later, the engine coughed its way down to 2000 rpm. It was then that I remembered that Joe had told me, "I sometimes have had to limp home slowly at below normal rpm." Slowly turned out to be eight or nine mph.

I had budgeted enough time to get to the boat yard in time to take the owner's twin daughters to lunch on their thirtieth birthday. This was a big mistake. Never make an appointment when depending on a 22-year-old boat. Two miles from my dock, the engine coughed to a complete stop. I knew I had plenty of gasoline, even though my broken gas gauge always reads empty.

It was a blazing-hot spring day and I forgot to bring along a hat or dark glasses, so I had to keep moving around in the shade of the small canvas cabin to protect myself from sunstroke. I was well aware that this kind of opening-day boating was a lot different than my yacht club days, days when I sailed a fast catamaran.

About this time, I managed to change the fuel filter without the proper tools, so then the engine ran great for about a hundred yards. Then, again, the engine coughed its way down to 1100 rpm and my speed dropped to 8mph. I was already an hour-and-a-half late for the birthday luncheon.

As I began to slowly turn left into Guemes Channel, I knew things were going to get worse because the outgoing tide was now running against me. It was time to get out my emergency outboard motor. It is very difficult to wrestle a 97-pound outboard motor onto a 12-inch bracket on the back of a small boat while it is rocking and rolling in a beam sea. I always keep a rope tied around the motor in case I drop it, so I will still have it attached to the boat. (It's not a case of *if* I drop it, but *when* I drop it.) The rope is just long enough to let me wrestle with the motor, but not so long that if I drop it, it will sink deep enough to completely disable it.

I managed to drop it this time and once again hauled it back on board. Then, after a struggle of what seemed like hours, I finally got the motor on the small bracket and tightened it down so it could help me get through my opening day of boating.

My outboard motor hadn't been used since last summer so, after about 300 yanks on the starting rope, I finally remembered to hook up the gas tank and it started right up. By now, the main engine on my boat had coughed and sputtered its way down to an insignificant 514 rpm and my speed was down to 4mph. The current was running against me at 3mph, so I headed for the lee shore to go against the slower current in the shallow water while hoping I didn't hit any rocks.

With the outboard racing at full throttle and the main engine running at 500 rpm, I was sitting on the transom in the blazing-hot sun, trying to steer the outboard. With both engines in my version of sync, I was able to get the boat up to 6mph through the water and 3mph over the bottom. It was during this time that I dinged the prop on a rock.

My noon-birthday luncheon date finally took

place at 3:55. It seemed as though the cold root beer, fish sticks, potato skins, and deep-fried Calamari hors d'oeuvres was the best opening day banquet I have ever tasted.

I miss the yacht club cannon shooting, but not all of the blue blazers, beehive hairdos, and speeches. This was, all things considered, a successful opening day for me, as I started the new season lurching from one near-disaster to the next.

A survival suit is similar to a pair of coveralls that are at least fourteen sizes too large.

FORTY-FIVE DEGREE
WATER IS COLD

The grocer here on my island almost lost his life recently when his small boat sank out from under him in a storm. Fortunately, he had a survival-suit on board and was able to climb into it before the boat dropped to the bottom of the sound in forty-five-degree water.

Since a survival suit saved his life, I thought it would be a good idea to buy two of them for my wife and myself. The water around here warms up to about fifty degrees in the summer; in the winter, it hovers around forty-three degrees. If you fall in, you have about twenty minutes before hypothermia sets in, where you can no longer function and simply drown.

Six hundred dollars later, the two survival-suits arrived via the local trucking company. I took them out of their bags and thought it would be a good idea to try one on in our living room before my wife and I had to climb into them on our boat in an emergency.

A survival suit is similar to a pair of coveralls that are at least fourteen sizes too large. Made out of very thick foam rubber, they have feet and hands attached, as well as a hood. When you finally get into one, all another person can see of you is about six square inches where part of your face is supposed to be. Assuming, of course, that you have put it on with the hands and feet pointing in the right direction, which I didn't do the first time that I tried to put mine on.

After about half an hour of trying to get into mine, I finally figured out that it would be a good idea if I took my shoes off first. Once I did that, it was fairly easy to dress for disaster. By the time I got the massive zipper pulled up and the Velcro seals all closed, I was already sweating and my wife was breaking up laughing at how I looked. When she finally got herself together, she said, "There's no way I'm going to look as dumb as you do in our living room. What if someone comes by and sees us? They'll call the police and have us both locked up."

Whereupon she got her camera and snapped a few shots of me looking exactly like Gumby, only in fire engine red. When she finally finished laughing, she said, "I'm going to the post office. Since this is an emergency drill, let's see if you can get out of that thing by yourself."

I couldn't.

The fingers of the gloves are also made out of quarter-inch, foam rubber and preclude any chance of being able to grab the toggle on a zipper and make it work. Remember the suits are designed for someone who weighs twice what you do, whatever size you are. That's so you can float around and take longer to die in cold Alaskan waters than if you just said, "This is it," and gave up.

Attached to the waist is a genuine police whistle. That's in case a policeman comes driving by after your boat sinks and while you are still alive and floating.

I was trying to get out of the suit ten minutes after Laurie left for the post office, when the Fed-Ex man showed up. I thought it would be dumb for him to see me sweating in a fire engine red, foam rubber suit, so I hid in the bedroom when he knocked on the door.

He finally drove away without my signature, so I came back out into the living room, still trying to unzip what had now become the survival-sweat-suit. By now, I was getting tired of standing up, but afraid to sit down. My clothes inside my red Gumby suit were wringing wet from sweating and I was now trying to get out of the suit any way I could. I found a pair of scissors I thought I could use, but the fingers on the gloves were too big to fit through the handles of the scissors.

I learned years ago to always try and stay calm in any life-threatening situation. By now, I had visions of the newspaper article, **"Film Maker found dead in a heap of foam rubber on his living room rug. Dehydration blamed."**

I finally took a calculated risk and fell down on the living room floor, knowing that my wife would be home from the post office in due time. I was trying to get comfortable lying down in my giant sweat-wet-suit that was only wet on the inside, when the phone rang. By the time I got to my feet and staggered over to try to answer it, the answering machine had taken over.

It was my wife.

"Hi, Warren. It's Laurie. I just ran into Grace at the post office and she has invited me into town for lunch. I hope you're out of your survival suit by now. I should be home in a couple of hours."

Click!

I wasn't out of it, I couldn't get out of it, and I didn't want to try to stagger up to the street and get some passerby to unzip me from this portable sauna. Instead, I thought, I might as well really test the suit, so I staggered down to our dock and flopped into the forty-three degree water.

The suit worked great. Except I forgot about the three-knot current flowing by our dock. I quickly drifted a couple of hundred yards west, and out into the main boating channel.

None of the passing boats stopped to rescue me.

I finally paddled ashore on our neighbor's, beach. Elmo's wife was having a bridge party on her deck and, when they saw this soaking wet, fire engine red monster, draped in seaweed and sand, stagger up over the bank from their beach, they all screamed and ran for the safety of the house. A few minutes later, I could hear the siren on the sheriff's car headed our way.

Twenty minutes after that, I had my survival suit under my arm and was walking down the road towards home. That's when my wife drove up and asked me what I was doing wandering around in broad daylight, all sweaty, with my new survival suit under my arm?

It seemed to me that the answer was obvious. I had just lurched away from my latest near-disaster!

SET YOUR ALARM FOR EARLY

My peripheral vision is cut down by about thirty percent because of an invention by an old friend of mine, Bob Smith. The white world has turned yellow as I look through his goggles while the heavy snowfall settles in my lap as I ride skyward with my friend Bruce Barr from San Juan Island.

It is 8:32 and I have been up since six. My six-year-old fat skis dangle from my new plastic boots as I glide up the mountain. Ahead of me, there are two chair-loads of skiers who beat us to being first in line.

No matter how many years I have been making turns, I still get excited when there is new powder snow covering the ten million ski tracks that have been laid down over the last week or so.

Scrunching down in my neck-gaiter and watching the trees alongside the trail pass by; the silence of the morning could be a religious experience for me.

If I was religious!

In less than five minutes, I will get to point my ugly, fat skis down a hill without a track. I can leave my tracks wherever I decide to ski.

It seems like only yesterday that my new fat skis made me ski as though I was 30 years younger. Sure, they are ugly, but I need all the help I can get. When they appeared on the market six or seven years ago, I was smart enough to buy a pair. All of the macho ski testers in Europe said, "They will never be a success," so they only shipped about forty pair into the United States that first year. In my

43

case, I paid full retail for my Atomic Fat Boys because I have had an attitude adjustment as the years rolled by when it relates to buying toys. In the early 1950's, I was the last guy in town to buy a pair of Head metal cheater skis. I was not going to make that same mistake twice. I have never looked back on my fat-ski decision. Yes, they are ugly and I have to use excuses whenever I ski in them. "They used to be a snowboard, but I hit it with my skill saw. I have a snowboard on each foot. They are an old man's skis, but I'm a fourteen-year-old kid trapped in a senior citizen's body."

The highlight of the day, once it stopped snowing, was to watch Bruce make the same number of linked turns in untracked powder to match his age. Then I had to do it because he did. We are all little kids when we have skis on. I have to tell you, 74 linked turns to match my age is a lot of linked turns.

By the end of the day, Bruce and I logged almost 40,000 vertical feet in untracked powder snow. Bruce is a decade or so younger than I am, but when we staggered back to our house we were both snoring on the couches within five minutes of when we sat down.

About noon during yesterday's powder snow day, I was riding up on the chair and looked down on the steep, gnarly, cut up, bump hill right under the lift. It hadn't been groomed all winter long and I thought:

That run, all random bumps, traverses, and junk is the way skiing used to be. It wasn't until 1954 or '55 after I had skied for 17 years, that a creative bulldozer operator in Aspen bolted some 2 x 4's to a very small Oliver tractor and started knocking down moguls that were so big you couldn't begin to see over them. I was upset about what he was doing to the ski run because I liked filming skiers with so many different choices of angles. I used to take shots when the skiers would appear, disappear, and then reappear again.

This was when Aspen only had two chairlifts and the lift lines were so long that I had to con my way to the head of the line to ride old #1. I always skied with my camera and skiers, so I could ride up and film on the way down. At the bottom, we would ski by some friends who I had left earlier and were still waiting in line. One powder snow day, I was making my third roundtrip of filming Herbert Jochum, who coached Andrea Mead Lawrence to her two Olympic Gold medals, when I passed some friends who were still waiting in the same line. They gave me a ration of dialogue that was hard to ignore.

But I did.

Those old days of waiting for as long as an hour or more to get on a single chairlift are a thing of the past. However, on a powder snow day like today was, detachable quads that haul over 2,500 people an hour to the top of a ski run can severely limit how many powder snow runs you can get before it is gone.

On a day like today, when it is snowing about an inch an hour and the wind at the top is blowing 10-to-25mph, there are occasional empty chairs. The only limit is your peripheral vision as you look at this wonderful white world through yellow goggles and feel the totality of rhythmic, powder snow turns. Often, in the middle of a powder snow run, I have to stop and ask no one in particular, "How come someone my age, or any age for that matter, is privileged to have this much fun?"

Just set your alarm for early.

"The
snow
will
come,
and
the
sun
will
shine,
and
isn't
that
enough?"

A FREEZING COLD
LOVE AFFAIR

Sometime when I was in junior high school or high school, in the late 1930's, my English teacher made me commit to memory this poem by Elizabeth Barrett Browning:

How do I love thee?
Let me count the ways,
I love thee to the depth and breadth
My soul can reach,
When feeling out of sorts.
And so on for a lot more stanzas...

I don't know why something that has been locked away in my brain for fifty or sixty years suddenly came to the surface the other day when I was riding up Chair Eight with my wife, Laurie, for the first time this year. It was a sunny day, no crowds, and someone had covered all of my favorite ski runs with great snow.

In my lifetime, I have had, like most people, a lot of love affairs, love affairs with a lot of different people, places, and things. My first one was with my roller skates that gave me my first taste of freedom. That is, once I figured out how to use them without falling. A few years, later along came my first bicycle, about the same time that a blonde in my seventh-grade geometry class appeared on the scene. I can't remember her name after all these years, but she made me aware that girls were certainly different than boys.

In 1937, I built a toboggan in my woodshop class, which led to me buying my first pair of skis for two dollars. That same year, I also built my first surfboard and managed to somehow catch a wave and stand up on it and ride the wave. A ride that lasted for twenty or thirty feet before I crashed in ankle-deep water on that awesome seven-inch-high wave.

I was head-over-heels in love with all of the above at various times in my life. As well as my first car, my first sailboat, my first still camera, and later my movie camera, salmon-fishing boat, and windsurfer. Today, as I look back on any one or all of them, each one of them gave me the same thing - a sense of freedom from the daily grind. Whatever it was at the time, selling magazines, a newspaper route, banging nails, digging ditches - it didn't matter; I still had my freedom toys.

Which is what that first chairlift ride of the year did the other day. It felt the same as every other first chairlift ride of the year since my first one in 1942, on Southern California's Mt. Waterman.

Love is a peculiar commodity. I have never been able to define it, and I know of no one else who can. I do know that there are unlimited numbers of things around a ski resort with which you can easily fall in love. The snow-grooming machines, the snow making machines, the quad chairs, the snow report, the mountain restaurants and the list continues to grow.

Hate, on the other hand, is another indefinable word. It was a lot easier for all of us when we had the Russians or the Germans to hate, because they threatened that basic instinct of ours - freedom.

Now that there is no major foreign government to turn our hatred toward, it is a lot easier to turn it towards things that affect our daily lives. These are things that we can't do anything about any more than we could, as an individual, do anything about the various wars we have lived through. I'm talking about things that are minor inconveniences, such as lift lines, or snow that is too deep, or not deep enough.

The other night my wife and I sat down and wrote up a list of things we really liked about living in a ski resort and another list of the things we hated about it.

When it got down to the push and shove of comparing our lists, about the only thing I could really gripe about was shoveling the driveway on a powder-snow morning. Which is really an absurd thing to gripe about because I don't do it. Instead, I go skiing.

In the last three months, I have visited a lot of cities with my new ski film. I have read about the drive-by shootings and all of the negatives of big-city living today. I have talked in person to tens of thousands of skiers who pay to come every year to see my new feature-ski film. I can say without a lot of argument that almost every single one of those people who come to my movie would like to move to a ski resort. The only reason they don't is economic. Many of them are working overtime so they won't have to wait until they are retirement age to buy their own house in Snow Country (so they can complain about shoveling out their own driveway).

By the time many of them are sixty years old, "down valley" will be a one or two-hour commute and they will have to live outside of the snow beltway. Which will give them something to complain about instead of their city commute.

In the first twenty years of my filming career, I climbed many mountains in many parts of the world and I learned, in a sweaty way, that any chairlift is an integral part of my ongoing love affair with the mountains. A love affair that once again blossomed and was even nicer, because I was able to make half a dozen runs on perfect snow with no one except my wife.

Laurie has promised that she will always wait for me at the lift when I want to take a cruiser instead of skiing at the speed that she cruises at. But then skiing is a big part of my love affair with life and with her in particular.

And I still can't define any of it.

I don't know why I feel like I do about ski lifts, but they let me ride up and ski down while I think about:

Hot chocolate and cookies; kids laughing in Fort Whipper-Snapper; semi-trucks lined up on I-70 in a blizzard; cars four-wheel drifting through the roundabout; groups of people disappearing in the snowflakes and darkness of the covered bridge; a Florida ski club dining on Pepi's porch in the spring sun; or the sound of Spanish amidst full-length mink coats at the grocery store.

Yes, there are a lot of reasons to be in love with a ski resort at this time of the year.

Editorial note: The 1950 Chevy van pictured on page 46 was Warren's home for the first three years of his film business. He had zero overhead while he continued his search for the free lift ticket.

A PRIVATE SKI RESORT

We were seated in the back of the plane. Fifteen feet in front of us, we could watch the right hand of a sixty-six year old, forty-five year veteran of flying, as he turned dials and switched switches. Then his hand moved to the throttles and, as he eased them back, we began the long decent to the runway. We had been cruising at 41,000 feet at 515 mph, and we could see the sun just going down behind the mountains that form Vancouver Island.

It had been a long day that started at 7am when we climbed into a single-engine tail-dragger for the short flight from our island home to Bellingham, Washington. There, we transferred to a Lear jet to fly to Truckee, California, and then on to Bozeman, Montana.

Sitting in the back of the plane with us from Truckee to Bozeman was the man who is rearranging mountains to create his own 13,000-acre ski resort. We were on our way to see what Tim Blixseth had done since I skied The Yellowstone Club with him last winter.

He has done a lot with his philosophy of doing it without borrowing money. He pays cash for everything.

He has carved out a eleven-mile road to Pioneer Peak that is somewhere between a two-lane road and a freeway, the first few miles of which are already paved. We didn't get to drive on the new road, however, because in Bozeman we transferred from the Lear Jet to a Llama helicopter for the short flight to his resort. Tim owns the full 13,000 acres and nothing he does to create the ideal ski resort requires the compulsory five years of hearings and endless trips to Washington, DC, to get permits to build a ski resort, as you must do on Forest Service land. (Or to build anything else nowadays.)

This will be the first major ski resort built in America in almost twenty years. After spending the day with the owner as our guide, I can assure you that everything he is doing to create this new ski resort, he is definitely doing right - ecologically, environmentally, and especially the manner in which he treats his employees.

There will be six chairlifts and a six-passenger gondola to get people up the hill so they can ski almost three thousand vertical feet of rolling terrain, not unlike Lionshead, Vail, and Seattle Ridge at Sun Valley. He even owns the backside of adjacent Lone Peak at Big Sky where he can, if he wants to, put up a lift and have wide-open bowls not unlike those at Sun Valley.

There were dozens of men on the mountain clearing trails and grinding the tree limbs into small chips to spread on the trails to encourage the future growth of vegetation. They had already stacked the bigger logs to build the log homes at the base, as well as the small cabins that will be tucked into glades around the mountain. A giant D-9 tractor was moving the rocks aside after we watched fifteen hundred pounds of dynamite explode under an outcropping of rock where too steep a pitch interrupted a long, cruising run.

Tucked off in the trees part way down the hill were seven log cabins under construction. These are the start of a small mountain village half way up the hill. These cabins are less than four hundred square feet, built entirely of logs, with a stone fireplace, a bathroom, a big porch, and a path to a larger lodge nearby. The larger building, about fifteen hundred square feet, will be the focal point of the seven cabins and will have a full-time chef-caretaker in attendance. He or she will cook your breakfast, lunch, dinner, or all of the above. Eventually, there will be one hundred of these cabins sprinkled around the mountain that a member of the Yellowstone Club can reserve for a night, a week, or all winter if they want to. But they won't be for sale.

Tim Blixseth has been in the timber business all of his life and he has learned what good and bad timber practices are and he is really caring for the environment in the ski resort he is creating.

He has a gondola, three snow cats, and detachable quads about ready for this winter's snow on 3,000 vertical feet of runs. The many runs he has cut this summer will be able to be skied in any and all kinds of snow conditions.

Tim could be likened to Averill Harriman who did a lot of things right when he invented Sun Valley, Idaho. Averill did this about the same time that metal edges for skis was invented in 1936. Tim has put together a group of very successful people for his advisory board and does something very unusual for a man in his position. As he said on the mountain. "I listen. That's why God gave us one mouth and two ears."

If all of this sounds too good to be true, there is always something hidden in the fine print of anything a person buys.

The fine print in this ski resort is that this will be a private club. That's right. A private club. To become a member will cost a seven hundred and fifty thousand dollars. A ridiculous price by most peoples' standards, but last spring a house in Aspen sold for $19,700,000. That's right; all of those numbers and zeros were on the check the buyer wrote. That amount of money is half of a basketball season's earnings for Michael Jordan or a week's pay for Bill Gates. I read recently where there are more than three million millionaires in America today. All Tim needs to find is one-tenth of one percent of them that would like to belong to a private ski club, and he is off and running. Oh yes, I forgot to mention that when you join The Yellowstone Club, there is an additional item called annual dues. This is a little over $2,000 a month, or $25,000 a year.

Perhaps this is where Michael Jordan, Bill Gates, Ivana Trump, or other highly visible celebrities can go skiing without being mobbed by the Paparazzi?

Will the Yellowstone Club be successful? I first skied it last March with a lot of skepticism. After spending a hot August day, yesterday: flying three thousand miles in two different airplanes, cruising above the mountain for an hour or so in a helicopter, seeing where Jon Reveal has laid out the trails and the lift lines, and listening to Tim explain how he was already handling almost every one of my, "Have you thought of?" ideas from my first visit last March, I came away with a very positive feeling for what he is doing.

Now, if I can somewhere, somehow come up with that initiation fee, I would seriously consider joining his club.

The wheels of the Lear Jet skidded on the runway at 125 miles an hour, reverse thrusters were activated and we came to a stop. Deplaning, we shook hands with Cecil our pilot, and Damon our co-pilot, and climbed back into the tail-dragging, single-engine airplane for the final twenty-mile flight to our island. There, we drove for fifteen minutes to our home on the south side of the island. (Five years ago, Laurie and I bought the property and converted a garage into a 900 square foot home.) It was almost dark when we walked into our living room and looked out at our dock with our small boat tied up to it, a boat I will go salmon fishing with in the morning.

Life is good. A boat to fish from, and a wife to cook the fish I catch in the garage we converted into our home. I have all of the freedom that I want, as well as an occasional ride in a private jet to a private ski resort.

It only took seventy-four years to earn this much freedom.

A portion of the 18,000 acre private Yellowstone Club ski resort near Bozeman Montana.

"I used to get a workout skiing down some of the race courses that I would film later. Today, I get a workout rowing my boat around some of the small islands where I live."

THE WORKOUT

Last winter, I purchased a beautiful new fiberglass rowboat so I could get some quiet exercise while rowing around the many islands that are near where we live in the summer. I could spot eagles, whales, and all sorts of wildlife as I rowed silently through the early morning light. I read all of the pamphlets, saw all of the videos at the January Boat Show, and settled on a modified Captain's Gig. At least that's what the brochure called it.

It is now officially called "The-muscle-breaker-blister-builder."

The other day I started out for my usual three-mile row around a nearby small island and made the mistake of going counter-clockwise instead of clockwise. At one point I had to go through a narrow pass and the tide was at full flood or about three or four knots. That's about five or six mph. It took me about twenty minutes to row upstream, but I hung in there and figured that on the way back I could coast almost all of the way home on the outgoing tide.

Wrong again!

I stopped on the far side of the island to see a friend of mine who is building a house and needed a hand moving some heavy lumber. By the time I got through helping him, the tide had really come in and my Captain's Gig was adrift at the far end of a long line in four feet of water. Fortunately, I had tied it to a tree branch that was on shore when I did it. So it was no big deal to walk out on the overhanging tree trunk and lower myself down into the boat. As I let go, headed for what was supposed to be the bottom of my Captain's Gig, I landed on the side of the boat.

It immediately capsized

I was instantly in 45-degree, waist-deep, freezing-cold water. At the same time, my oars were floating away, and I now had to retrieve them from chest-deep water. Then I got to wade ashore and drag the boat behind me. My now-former friend, who I had just helped with all of his lumber, was laughing so hard he was no help at all. My dog Pepper was barking and generally getting in the way. He was at least dry for now.

A fourteen-foot rowboat full of what seems to be about twenty-thousand gallons of water is no mean trick to bail out in the fast-fading light when you are sopping wet and freezing cold. I finally got everything back in order and I thought the two-mile row home with the tide would be a breeze and would keep me warm enough until I got there.

Wrong again!

The tide had shifted, and I had to row uphill all the way home. Instead of twenty or thirty minutes of exercise, it took almost an hour. When I finally started across the bay in front of our house, it was pitch black.

My wife, Laurie, had all the lights that aren't burned out on the porch turned on, so in the darkness I had some sort of target to row toward.

My dog was shivering almost as much as I was by now, and trying to snuggle up to me for warmth. This makes rowing a little difficult with a 25-pound dog in your lap who is also whining and shaking. The blisters on my hands were the only warm part of me as I finally made it back to my dock.

I came in on the wrong side of it and the current kept pushing me away from it. My numb brain finally figured that out, and I rowed around to the other side. My new Captain's Gig now banged against the dock because of the current, so Pepper jumped out and ran for the warmth of the house.

This left me all alone in the dark to unship the oars, and then try to climb out of the boat. About four percent of the muscles I owned still worked. I finally took a chance and somehow managed to stand up in the rowboat and, fortunately, fell over onto the dock.

We get a lot of wind and rain where we live, so I couldn't leave the boat in the water overnight. I had to drag it up onto the dock. This took whatever I had left in me, but I finally staggered up towards the house.

Inside were three couples that I had forgotten we were having over for a welcome-home-for-the-summer dinner party. I was two hours overdue and Laurie had already called the sheriff, the Coast Guard, and every neighbor within three miles.

Once I warm up, which will take about a week or so, I'm going to spend the next three days working in my shop to build some outriggers for my new rowboat so it won't tip over in the future. I think I'm going to put outriggers on both sides. I can do that, or I can practice walking on slimy, horizontal, tree trunks over freezing cold water.

When you are retired, you have a lot of options about HOW to get a workout.

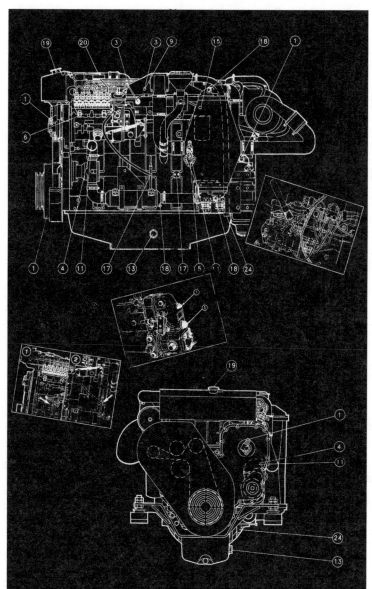

"I didn't know a fuel pump from a propeller. And I wouldn't be surprised if these were drawings for a diesel engine instead of an outboard motor."

THE FUEL PUMP

The hot sun is beating down on my sunburned back as I nurse the Pursuit up to the dock in Mosquito Pass on the north end of San Juan Island. For the last twenty miles or so, the 175 H.P. Johnson on the transom has been cutting out, so we finally feel safe here at the dock. Our friends, Bruce and Becky Barr, live here and own this dock. He is a commercial fisherman and knows all about motors; besides, we need to use their hot shower and washing machine for a couple of hours.

It is soon obvious why they call it Mosquito Pass, as two hundred and fifteen million of the suckers smell fresh blood that is now available in my two-hundred-and-something-pound body.

By the time my wife, Laurie, and I have on the mosquito repellent, at least fifty of them are so full of blood that their aerodynamic capacity is severely hampered and, instead of flying, they have to walk home.

The mosquito repellent smells like a combination of lemon-flavored furniture polish, saltwater soap, and kerosene. When it dries, it feels like caked-on mud.

By the time Bruce ambles down the dock to greet us, I have out my bible of cruising in a small boat, "REPAIR AND MAINTENANCE OF THE 175 H.P. JOHNSON OUTBOARD" (Volume 19, 1980 through 1983).

I had already turned to the trouble-shooting pages when Bruce said,

"Sounded like your fuel pump was acting up when you came into the dock."

He then introduced me to his neighbor who had motored over from his own private island in his small outboard motorboat with his son, so they could drive into Friday Harbor and pick up some stuff.

At the house, Bruce phoned the local outboard motor guru and, yes, he allowed as he had a pair of fuel pumps, but he was backlogged two weeks on boat repairs.

"Did I think I could install them myself?"

"Why not?"

Now I am riding to Friday Harbor in an ancient pickup truck of unknown vintage or origin. Any identifying marks have long ago rusted and fallen off on the road somewhere. The front of the cab is held together by the recent addition of some not-yet-too-rusty bailing wire and, in the back with me, are three crab traps, one Labrador Retriever, what's left of a bundle of shingles, and a rusty bicycle. We all are bouncing around as we head for Friday Harbor to pick up the fuel pumps and some groceries for the man from the other island. (The rusty bicycle is to ride home on when the truck breaks down. Which it does regularly, evidently).

I know it is going to be a long trip when, about two miles from Mosquito Pass while we are laboring up a long hill, three people riding bicycles pass us.

Real trouble. I could tell because one of them was a brain-bucketed, Lycra-clad, senior citizen who was riding an eighteen-speed mountain bike with three wheels and towing a trailer with her grandchild in it.

The ten-mile trip took a little over an hour.

The head of the parts department at the combination marina, hamburger stand, gift shop, fishing guide headquarters and Seven-Eleven store is also a real estate agent. We had to wait for him to get back from a four-martini sale on a two-acre parcel in the center of the island.

"Yep, here they are. Got just two of them left and the numbers almost match the ones you want. Better take them and try them; otherwise, I have to phone Seattle for exactly the right kind. Then they have to ship them to Anacortes by way of Bellingham on the Greyhound bus. Then they have to come up on the ferry from there. You can figure on three or four days at least."

These are last year's prices on the box, but this year's prices have only gone up a little bit."

A little bit was 40%.

"We always charge a little more if you are using a credit card."

I finally have them and now it seems like a dozen more stops in the ancient, rusty pickup truck before we can head back to Mosquito Pass by way of the eight-mile, winding road.

The right rear spring long ago had broken under the ravages of rust and overloading, and new shocks are something you get in this part of the world when you rent a horror movie for your VCR.

Every time we came to a curve that even looked like it was going to veer to the left, we had to slow down to about three or four miles an hour. The sixteen-mile round-trip took several hours, and now it was time to get down to the serious business of the replacing of the fuel pumps.

"Let's see the directions."

"Oops! The serial numbers on the pumps are not the same serial numbers as they say they are on the boxes."

"They look the same."

Bruce, in his wisdom of many years of commercial fishing, said,

"Warren, don't worry. Just unhook the gas line first and then replace both of the pumps because they look alike and it should work fine."

I did all of the above and it wouldn't start.

"Why don't you put a new pump on the top station and use the old one on the bottom?"

I did and it still didn't start.

"Why don't you put a new pump on the bottom station and leave the old one on the top?"

I did and it still didn't start.

"Why don't you put a different new one on the top and start the whole cycle of changing pumps again, only this time in reverse order?"

After several more hours, replacing fuel pumps, I had nothing to show for it except greasy hands and twelve thousand mosquito bites because, when you sweat, the repellent washes off with the sweat. Oh, yes, I also had a boat battery that was rapidly running down.

Laurie and Becky returned from lunch to sit chatting with us while Laurie applied more mosquito repellent to my now very swollen body. By now, the Island visitor had long ago gone back to his private island. Bruce was getting bored with the whole fuel-pump-replacement-process and getting ready to tow me to Friday Harbor for a major overhaul.

Laurie offered to make us an afternoon snack of come cold cracked crab and a cold drink.

I accepted and, as I was replacing an old fuel pump with a new fuel pump on the bottom station, Laurie said,

"Do you suppose it would run if you hooked up the gas line?"

I did and it did.

A FRIEND OF THE
FATHER OF THE BRIDE

A few months ago, I made the mistake of volunteering to help my friend Dick with his daughter's wedding. He has a house on an island nears ours that has no regular Washington State ferry service. Since I have a twenty-foot boat that can haul eight or ten passengers at a time, I was one of the logical people to haul as many of his wedding guests as possible from our island to their island.

The day of the wedding started with all of the normal confusion. A reported 160 guests would have to be ferried from one of three places - the commercial ferry landing, two miles away, a float plane dock the same distance away in another direction, and The Deer Harbor Marina in a third direction. Once we got the people to Crane Island, they would somehow have to get the two miles to the wedding site. Which was a sort-of brand-new two-thirds finished house overlooking a beautiful stretch of Wasp Passage.

Picking up the guests started when the first float plane arrived at 9:00 A.M. Those passengers were taken to The Deer Harbor Marina to change clothes and maybe catch a salmon or two while they waited for the ceremony. Next was the 10:05 ferry that didn't arrive until 11:10. Twenty-six people had to be taken to the Marina. The mother of the bride called my wife and asked if we could pick up a few bags of ice.

We got eight just in case.

The grand plan was to transport all of the guests to the smaller island between 3:30 and 4:00, so they could walk or hitchhike the two miles to the wedding site in their dressed-for-the-city-wedding-silk-summer-dresses, high heel pumps, or coats, ties and Gucci loafers, without socks

(It's not fashionable to wear socks with loafers to a summer wedding in the woods on an island.)

Between 12:00 and 12:30, our boats had to pick up: the caterer and all of her pots, pans, plates, and stuff; six wait persons; a six-foot-long barbecue for the roast beef, and salmon; and an, "Oh by the way, will you pick up forty more bags of ice on your next trip?"

Once I bought and loaded the 200 pounds of ice, I stopped by my own dock to pick up the disc jockey and a big bag of extra CD's that she had forgotten. (She had also forgotten to go to weight watchers for the last eleven years, but fortunately my boat has trim tabs.)

In the meantime, the word was out that the bag pipe player who was going to play the wedding march had run out of gas in his 1963 Volvo and was last seen hitchhiking. No one would pick him up in his Tartan-plaid mini-skirt, long socks, and white spats.

The vocalist showed up who had also missed the last nineteen years of Weight Watchers. (We knew the ceremony would be over when she sang.)

We somehow got all of them to the small island and now it was time to pick up the groom and his half a dozen ushers at the Marina while the other two boats started ferrying the many guests. In a short period of time, almost two hundred guests had to be moved in three, twenty-foot boats. That's a lot of trips in overcrowded boats.

After spending three hours at the hairdressers, the bridesmaids arrived at the island in yet another boat, went to a neighbor's house to get dressed, and then climbed into a four-passenger, electric golf cart similar to the ones they use in large motels to drive around flat parking lots.

The first hill the cart came to, the bridesmaids and then the bride had to get out and walk. The cart wouldn't even climb the hill with just the driver. He had to hold the throttle down with one foot and hop along beside it on his other foot. At the same time, the bridal party struggled up the hill with their long dresses up above their knees in order to keep them out of the ankle-deep dust. In places, the road was too rocky to walk barefooted, so it was high heels and good looking legs staggering along behind the cart. At the top of the hill, everyone climbed back into the cart and sped to the wedding site. Once there, the brakes weren't strong enough to stop it, as they headed down the narrow path to the two-thirds fin-ished, new house. They careened right on by and after skidding across the crooked dance floor, came to a semi-abrupt stop against the disc jockey's col-lection of about ten thousand CD's.

I was picking up the last of the people who arrived on the 2:10 ferry that finally arrived at 3:45, when I got the message that the caterer had forgot-ten the knives, forks, and spoons. My wife Laurie got on the phone and located some at the ferry landing and some at the Marina, so another pair of trips was in order.

In the meantime an eighty-eight-year-old grandmother was driven across the small island to the ceremony on the back of her daughter's power lawn mower.

A man who owns a farm on the island hitched up his hayrack to his John Deer tractor and hauled people from the dock to the ceremony. Gucci shoes, blue blazers, silk dresses, straw and hayseed went well together.

As I drove my boat back to my dock for the twenty-third time so I could take a shower and later help my daughter take some wedding pictures, I saw that one of the other boats had run out of gas. So I towed him to where a five-gallon can of gas had been stashed. Since three or four ferries had been late, the mother of the bride had wisely postponed the wedding for one hour.

I showered, picked up my wife and the last two guests who were staying in our guest tent, and we arrived at the ceremony to the wonderful sounds of the guy in the plaid mini-skirt playing what was supposed to be the wedding march on his bagpipes. I found out later that it was the same tune that a bag piper had played when the Scotch Highlanders were fighting the Battle of the Shirts near Fort William Scotland in 1342.

It was a great way to start a wedding.

The ushers and the bridesmaids were now marching down the gravel path to where the lady judge would perform the ceremony. When they got there, the fugitive from Jenny Craig sang a very emotional song that sounded beautiful set against the backdrop of Wasp Passage, as the ferryboat steamed by and honked SOS on its foghorn. The bagpipe player couldn't hear her sing and was playing his song in a different key and to a different rhythm.

During the ceremony, the judge used the wrong names and tried to marry the bride to her father instead of the groom.

To the endless clicking of cameras, it was now time for the champagne toast all around and then the dreaded dance of the father of the bride with the mother of the groom and vice versa. At that precise moment, the disc jockey decided to play some garage band music that sounded like a sack of cats on the way to the river.

As soon as the dance was over, everyone split for some fabulous salmon and roast beef. The first 160 people ate all of the food and the last, unplanned-for, 40 guests got to eat what was left of the corn bread and sliced tomatoes. However, each of them also got a chit from the father of the bride that was good for a pair of Big Macs, two orders of fries, and a pair of chocolate shakes at the other end of the Ferry boat ride on the way home.

At 8:30, on an island half a mile away, someone got in their boat and rowed over and demanded that the disc jockey turn the music off because his wife went to bed at 8:30 on Saturday nights. (She'd be loads of fun to live with!)

At 9:30, it was now time to begin evacuating the island. The farmer ran out of gas in his John Deere tractor and no one else could get past on the one-lane dirt road with the other vehicles to haul the guests to the dock and the boats.

Everyone walked.

At 11:00, the fiancée of one of the boat drivers fell into the water when she was trying to go potty and hanging over the back of the boat. The other boat driver had taken his last load of passengers to the 10:00 o'clock ferry for the mainland and ran out of gas on the way back. He drifted around for two hours in the dark without lights or flares on his boat. He did have a black life jacket to wear, however. He finally drifted within shouting range of some kayakers who were camped on the beach. They paddled out, towed him ashore, and gave him some gas from their camp stove. It was enough to get his boat back to my dock where he had left his car, so he called it a night.

The next morning, I picked up the bride and groom, took them to their 8:30 floatplane, and went back and took a nap. At 9:30, there were nine more trips back and forth to the ferry for the people who stayed overnight. Later in the afternoon, I drove my boat over to Anacortes with my wife for a much-needed, quiet dinner. About four hundred yards from the dock, I ran out of gas.

I had to paddle my twenty-foot, three-thou-sand-pound boat the last four hundred yards and Laurie and I missed our dinner reservations by half an hour. Every restaurant in town was sold out until 9:30, so I got to use those Big Mac chits that the father of the bride had given me when I missed dinner at the wedding.

RANDOM NOTES
FROM SOMEWHERE

I was thumbing through some of my old notes this morning and came across a few observations from some of my trips. My travel notes are exactly like those on my check stubs. Blfsk, Frws, Opac, and other such scribbling as though from a less intelligent being from a galaxy far, far away. They're written on an assortment of old napkins, place mats, an occasional paper plate, match book covers, You name it, I've made notes on it.

I knew what I was going to write about at the time the notes were made, a month ago, a year ago, even a decade or more ago. Here's one: DC-3 Miami-LAX 1944 means it was a two-day flight from Miami to Los Angeles in 1944. I slept overnight on the floor of the tail-dragger airplane while the crew got to sleep in the last room available in a five-dollar-a-night motel at the airport in Houston. The floor of the plane was on such a steep angle that I kept sliding down towards the tail and waking up in the bathroom.

More random note interpretations from somewhere, sometime:

♦ With dinner entrees starting at $30.95 you would think that the guy sitting at the next table would be sophisticated enough to take off his baseball hat. Or at least wear it frontwards.

♦ Why is it that some men with four pockets in their pants still wear a fanny pack and use it as a purse? When they sit down they have to pull the purse around to their stomach so they look fat enough to be the captain of the Ajax Brewery bowling team. At least I thought he had a fanny pack on under his shirt.

♦ There is something incongruous about a man who is six foot three that weighs two hundred and twenty-seven pounds, with a long scraggly beard wearing dangling turquoise earrings.

♦ Shining in the orange glow of a Maui sunset, her face was a beautiful testimony to the skill of her plastic surgeon.

♦ Why is it that no matter what airport I arrive at, there are at least three hundred and fifty-three luggage carts I can rent, but the one that I always get has a wobbly wheel?

♦ President Clinton was three years old when I produced my first feature-length ski film. Today, he is five!

♦ I took still photos of guests on the Squaw Valley porch when I was teaching skiing there in 1949/50. I would process them at night and sell an 8x10 print the next day for a dollar. If the lady in the photograph were not the man's wife, I would sell him the negative for $5.

♦ Twenty years ago, you could smoke anywhere on an airplane. Since I have never smoked, I would always wind up seated next to an Eastern

European who smoked cigarettes that smelled like burning CAMEL DUNG. Occasionally, one of them would be polite enough to ask; "Do you mind if I smoke?" My standard answer? "Go right ahead, as long as you don't mind if I throw up."

♦ In Philadelphia during a live narration of my film, I heard a gasp from someone in the balcony. Amidst a lot of confusion, two couples got up and hurriedly left the theater. I found out after the show that one of the ladies who left was pregnant and had her baby on the way to the hospital while I was showing the second reel. She blamed the three-day premature birth of her child on the fact that I had laughed it out of her.

♦ An ad in the Truckee, California, newspaper dated February 1950: **Squaw Valley view lots $1,000.** (That's one thousand dollars.) My paycheck was $125 a month so I didn't buy one.

♦ Original limited partnership offerings to buy part of Vail in 1961 were **Mill Creek Circle lots with two, lifetime, lift passes for $10,000.** In 1993, one of those $10,000 lots with the original $20,000 house on it was sold for five and a half million dollars. Yes, there can be a future in ski resort investments.

♦ New Zealand, 1968. I saw volcanic rocks that float and logs that are such hard wood that they sink. I swam in water so clear that it was almost invisible. The volcanic lake at the top of Mt. Ruapehu had changed since my last visit, from a snow-rimmed 103-degree Fahrenheit lake that was a delight to swim in to one with such a high sulfuric acid content that even the volcanologists could no longer paddle their boat in it.

♦ Historical trivia about the same volcano. Many years ago one rim of the lake melted out and the lake poured down the side of the mountain in a massive flood. It roared down a dry riverbed and wiped out a railroad trestle just as the southbound train to Christchurch was crossing it on Christmas Eve. All the passengers perished.

♦ My plane from San Francisco to Salt Lake City had to circle for an hour and a half over Winnemuca, Nevada, while President Ford, with his Air Force One parked at the gate, gave a speech at the University of Utah. (I couldn't use the same auditorium to show my ski movie until he finished his speech anyway, so it was no big deal.)

♦ Magnetic safety bindings. I told Ivan that his invention was a good one. He had a battery on his belt, magnets in his boots, and a metal plate on his wooden skis, that had a light corduroy texture to it. When torque was applied to the boot in a fall, the magnetic field would be disrupted and the ski would come off. When I posed the question, "What are you going to do about the magnetized ski sticking to the footrest of the chair lift?" his reply was, "I never thought of that."

♦ Power Skis: Don Voorhees had chain saw motors driving an endless caterpillar tread in each ski, a five gallon can of gas in his rucksack, and a throttle in each ski pole handle. No more lift tickets to buy. When he got to the top of the hill, the ski would be turned upside down and he could then

74

ski down. He had already perfected the binding that would revolve through a horizontal axis. His market would be the United State Army. When I mentioned that a platoon of soldiers with a chain saw motor on each ski would have a hard time sneaking up on the enemy. He said, "I am also working on a muffler for the engines."

♦ Is it possible that most of the liberal judges in America today were at Woodstock together?

♦ I was filming a promotional movie for the Inertia Ski Binding Company to demonstrate how safe their new radical bindings were. The skier demonstrating the bindings for my camera fell and broke his leg. The ski resort's press release about the accident scared away any potential investors.

♦ An invention I have in the works: I am making fortune cookies out of pretzel dough, putting dirty jokes in them, and selling them in bars? Why not?

The sport of mountain biking has escalated to where it's not for the faint-of-heart, but for the fat-of-wallet.

MOUNTAIN BIKE MANIA
INVADES SKI RESORTS

There was a time, not so long ago, when the wildflower pickers and the tree huggers could enjoy a quiet, leisurely climb alone to the summit of Mt. Baldy.

Those days are gone, as fat-tire aficionados are sweating and grunting their way to that same summit on their state-of-the-art mountain bikes. The smart ones can spend five dollars and get a ride to that same summit on the chair lift or gondola with their exotic fat-tire vehicle dangling from a hook on the back, like a dead $1253 marlin in Cabo San Lucas.

The sport of mountain biking has escalated to where it is not for the faint-of-heart, but rather for the fat-of-wallet.

A fat-tire, 18-speed, top-of-the-line, XYZ-brand bike can cost anywhere from $300, to as much as $6,000. Yes, even more if you want those thirty-four coats of hand-rubbed lacquer, instead of a Zolatone finish. (Zolatone is that splash of different colors of paint that looks like the ancient elementary schools of by-gone eras. Schools that were Zolatoned so that the dirt and marks of the hundreds of gremlins attending school wouldn't show.)

You will also need several pair of contrasting-colored Spandex shorts at $75 a pair. You will wear out the fanny in them before you wear out your enthusiasm for this new "the mountain-is-free" sport.

You will need a streamlined brain-bucket to

decrease wind resistance and to save your life during the many falls you will be taking once you decide to become a racer. A good brain-bucket will cost between $50 and $100, depending on its color and how much room it has for billboard-type advertising decals.

Add to the total so far, a range of colorful jerseys that are usually adorned with foreign words that no one comprehends unless they, too, are fat-tire aficionados. They usually spell the name of some intergalactic champion of some kind and his hometown or country of origin, which you have never heard of. An adoring crowd will ask you what each word means every time you stop at a pub on the way home from your sweaty, dusty, bike ride. You will usually stop to replenish the gallons of body fluids you have passed through your pores on your laborious climb to the top of the mountain to save the five-dollar lift ride fee.

Question: How do you get anything out of the pockets of the jerseys when they are in the back?

And, finally, you will need a special pair of darling-looking dancing shoes that slip into the slots on the special, expensive pedals of the lightweight, special alloy crank on your super-lightweight bike.

These shoes don't have any heels, so that when you're walking in them, they make you walk just the opposite of how you would walk in a pair of cowboy boots. It is as though you have a one-inch high heel nailed to the toe of each shoe and the only way you can keep from falling backwards is to walk with you feet pointing out to the side. But that's O.K. because you look lovely with your legs shaved so that there is very little wind resistance as you walk along, shoving your bike with the flat tire.

Extra weight on your bicycle is extra time you'll have to spend riding back and forth to the same place. Shaving weight from your titanium alloy steed will probably cost from $25 to as much as $100 an ounce.

Going on that postponed diet would be a lot cheaper.

You will also need a water bottle that slips into a lightweight holder somewhere on the frame of your bike. These water bottles have been known to carry every type of liquid that is drinkable by man.

Now that you are fully equipped, you can't just go out and ride this magnificent feat of engineering. Each time you ride, you have to exceed your own personal best by some imagined, self-imposed, percentage. If you are unable to do that, your entire day is wasted and you will spend the rest of the day beating yourself up over your lack of personal improvement.

Vertical footage per hour versus mileage is always carefully computed against your heart monitor and your oxygen-usage meters, which are strapped to your body and register somewhere on your handlebars.

"It took you how long to go how high and how far?"

The first liar doesn't have a chance.

Now that I own a mountain bike, occasionally my wife and I will put them in the back of the van and drive up the highway to the summit of a nearby pass, or to the top of anywhere a paved road might go. We'll ride a hundred yards or so away from the highway and have a delightful picnic out in the woods while resting from the long hard drive. Then we'll start coasting back down the highway, or perhaps down a wonderful asphalt bicycle path that was built for about $843,000. The ride, or rather the coasting back to where we have our other car parked, takes about half an hour or so. While that is happening, I really enjoy the wind whistling through the threads of my Levi's and the holes in my brain-bucket where the duct tape has fallen off.

Once we get to the other car, we will drive back up and retrieve our van and drive home in a caravan.

When I decided to become a fat-tire aficionado, I shopped around for a long time to find a good one. The cheapest (interpreted in my mind as good) one I could find in the specialty-bike shop was $475. Then, one day it happened. I was in Wal-Mart, shopping for a new fly rod, some flies, a reel, and some line, when I wandered through their toy department and there it was. The top-of-the-line, most expensive mountain bike they had in the store was $235. I bought two of them on the spot, one for me and one for my wife. She was less than thrilled. They came in an assortment of contrasting Zolatone colors, which I thought *should* have made her even happier.

The low price even included a water bottle and a brain-bucket. The only thing I had to do was assemble the bicycles. I was told that they would assemble them for me for an additional ten dollars each. I decided to splurge and let them do it!

With the money I saved, my wife and I can ride up on the ski lift and coast back down all summer long and still have some money in the bank.

My next purchase will probably be a rucksack, so I can ride to the nearby convenience store. It is somewhere between seven and eleven vertical feet higher than where we live, so I know I'm getting good exercise for my oxygen-usage meter. And, I'll be able to coast all the way home!

WITHDRAWAL

Many times I've been asked the question, "What would you be doing if skiing had never been invented?"

This winter, I have been finding out the hard way.

In September, I started the long haul of trying to beat my tired old body back into shape so I could enjoy skiing as soon as we returned to the mountains. I was doing all of my sport-cord exercises, knee-sits against the wall, that sort of thing, and decided to do a few push-ups. No big deal! Two days later, I repeated my new exercise program and discovered, to my amazement, that I could not do one single push-up. It was not pretty. My body would not leave the floor.

Many, many dollars later, spent on MRIs, x-rays, and several visits to local doctors in Seattle, I flew to Vail and discovered what I feared I had done. I had torn my rotator cuff. Again. The left one, this time.

By doing push-ups? Give me a break! When Dr. Hawkins said,

"If we repair it right now, I can have you skiing by the beginning of February," I thought, what the heck. I could miss skiing in December and January and still have 90 skiing-days lift before the lifts shut down.

I was operated on the next morning.

The rehab on my shoulder was going well when, on about the tenth of January, the new mutated blend of Chinese Flu, Japanese Crud, Mexican two-step, was mixed up with equal parts of Los Angeles smog and some of Saddam's biological weaponry brought aboard an airplane in which I was riding. Within hours, it had me laid out like some 29-day-old road-kill.

Each day blended into the next for me, while I spent my time constantly coughing. My friends called and reported,

"Wow! You really missed it in the back bowls today!"

"Blue River has never been so good. Seven days of cobalt-blue skies and new snow every night!"

I now know what it must be like to withdraw from drugs or alcohol. I have found out just how addicted I have been most of my life. Addicted to the freedom I enjoy when I ski down the side of a hill much faster than anyone my age should be going.

People told me,

"Go to Arizona and thaw out, get some sun in your face."

But living at the base of a ski lift in Colorado, I keep thinking I might miss that perfect-powder snow day. At the same time, I have to weigh what the doctor says about the stupidity of risking tearing my shoulder up, once again. But this time, at least, I would tear it up skiing.

In the old days, in Europe, the only cure for tuberculosis, influenza, bronchitis, and other respiratory ailments was to get up into the Alps for the pure air and sunshine. Instead, while lying flat on my back under the humidifier and in serious withdrawal, I have tried to pass some of the time analyzing the 114 different news programs on satellite TV, Saturday morning cartoons (yes, I've been that desperate), never-before-heard-of-colleges playing basketball, and CBS Olympic advertising.

For the last sixty years, I have managed to ski at least ten or twelve days a winter and sometimes as many as two hundred. My days have been spent skiing, filming, and traveling. When, and if, I got this same respiratory problem, I would just stop at some doctor's office where, for $10, I could get a shot of penicillin. Then in a couple of hours, I would feel good enough to, once again, sit up in the car and drive to my next filming job, personal appearance lecture, or meeting.

Now that my forced, but temporary, withdrawal from the ski scene has stuck me with television news that has been influenced so much by the right-wing conspiracy theories of Hillary's, I would like to offer another theory:

Is it possible that Saddam Hussein is directly responsible for my current major attack of the Iraqi bronchial flu? Has he been manufacturing this hybrid respiratory strain so that people such as myself will be stricken down and forced to watch the chair lift run all winter without ever riding up the mountain?

Sixty years of pursuing the wonderful habit (addiction?) of skiing is a long time. Slowly, I'm watching my first winter of non-skiing since 1937 drag by, trying to find some way to cope with my life without it. My shoulder won't let me ski, I can't even go windsurfing or play golf, and my lungs only let me cough. Whatever germ warfare Saddam is spraying into airplane ventilating systems might be a very real CNN evening news item.

I'll be sure to watch this fast-breaking, biological warfare story on TV while curled up in bed with my eye on the tube, wondering how Saddam knew how and when to tear my rotator cuff?

I know that as soon as the defense department gets to the bottom of this biological-warfare flu problem of Saddam's, I'll be back out there, making turns on my skis and every day of the year, somewhere in the world, it is snowing, and isn't that enough?

"Somewhere in the world it is snowing, and isn't that enough?"

A LOT OF BULL

    I live on an island that takes as long to get to from Seattle in a car and a ferryboat as it does to get to Chicago in a Boeing 737. I live there for a lot of reasons, one of which, are the interesting people I meet on the ferryboat.

    On the ferryboat are all kinds of cars, trucks, people, trailers, kayaks, backpackers, salesmen, real-estate agents, bicycles, property buyers, and occasionally some livestock.

    The other night, my neighbor Clyde and his wife Yvonne stopped by and asked me if I would help him fill out an insurance claim for automobile damage to his 1949-Studebaker truck that occurred on a recent ferryboat ride.

    He was parked on the lower level, half-asleep, when a lot of hooting and hollering woke him up. He's kind of a nosey guy, so he sat up and looked out the windshield just as the three ferryboat car-parkers came running by in their light-up-in-the-dark, orange vests. They sounded like a bunch of drunken cowboys heading for a Saturday night brawl.

    They had just finished running by the car when they came running back the other way, only faster.

    Clyde is kind of slow moving because he has only one leg. Sometimes, his 40-year-old prosthesis locks up due to the damp air and a touch of rust, so it's sort of hard for him to get out of the truck. So he rolled down the window and was surprised to note that a very large calf or yearling heifer was chasing the car-parkers. No matter its age, it seemed big and was running hard.

Since Clyde's truck was about in the middle of the ferryboat, he was afraid that the car-parkers might forget and run off the bow of the boat into the frigid water of the Northwest and get run over by the ferryboat. For fifteen dollar-an-hour car-parkers, these guys were still able to dodge and weave and not disappear off the bow.

It seems that the young heifer was a bull and the orange vests were working just like a Spanish bullfighter's red cape. That young bull, which can usually stop in about two bull-lengths, slid five-and-a-half bull-lengths when he tried to stop on the metal deck of the ferryboat. He spun around and once again started running back down the aisle between Clyde's truck and the car alongside.

About the fourth trip down the length of the ferryboat by the guys who were running away from the bull, the galloping bull, and the guys who were running after the bull, Clyde decided he could do something to help out. By this time he had gotten his prosthesis working, so he figured that the next time the car-parkers who were running away from the bull ran by his car, he would time things just right and open his car door before the bull was scheduled to run by. Then, if someone behind opened their car door, they would have the bull cornered and the car-parkers could tie him up and get him back into the bull owner's truck.

As I said, Clyde is a little slow in his thinking process, so he opened the truck door when the four-hundred-pound bull was running wide open down between the line of cars.

A four-hundred-pound bull, galloping along on

the steel deck of a ferryboat with his head down, has enough energy going his way to bend a 1949-Studebaker door inside out.

That bull did just that. He bent it double. Right back against the left front fender. Which is why Clyde wanted me to help him with his insurance claim.

After the bull hit the door, he just kind of staggered around like a punch-drunk fighter. Before the car-parkers could tie him up, he wandered off the back of the ferryboat and started swimming. Apparently the cold water took away his headache and he started swimming like crazy, but in the wrong direction.

Now the ferryboat captain with his load of several hundred life-endangered souls on board had to stop the boat and put a lifeboat over the side to try and herd to bull to the nearby beach.

The ferryboat-car-parkers are not very good at rounding up swimming bulls, even when they are small, so this took another twenty minutes before they could get the bull swimming toward the right island. There, it was finally captured (rounded up) by eleven volunteer firemen, two paramedics, and one sheriff.

How do you explain some cowhide buried on the inside of a bent double door for a 1949-Studebaker pickup truck and make the insurance investigator believe the story?

Even more important, where will Clyde find a left-hand door for a 1949-Studebaker pick-up truck, even if the insurance investigator believes his story? Which he won't! As I said, it's a lot of bull!

The Sun Valley Ski School staff, 1948/49. With their spiffy over-the-socks, pleated-in-the-front, hip hugger pants. Left to right in the front row: John Litchfield, Floyd Dupuis, Joe Ward, Director Otto Lang, Florian Hammerli, Charlie Cole, Bill Butterfield, Sigi Engl. Second row: Andy Henning, Yves Latrielle, Emile Allais, Yvonne Tache, Dave Brandt, and Adolph Rubishek. Third row: Sepp Froehlic, Leon Goodman, Karl Hinderman, Fritz Kramer, and Wendy Cram. Fourth row: Les Outs, Kenny Zimmerman, Robert Albuoy, Glen Young, and Warren Miller, who supplied everyone with his homemade nylon-parachute-shroud-shoelaces at a 50% discount.

SKIING WITH THE SHAH

In Deer Valley, Utah, a couple of weeks ago, I was listening to the crackling of hand-held radios being used by Clinton watchers. They were all trying to locate Chelsea and Hillary on their $3,700,000 (that's million, folks) learn-to-ski weekend. It made me think about a similar incident with a head of state in Sun Valley, Idaho, many years ago.

The Shah of Iran had come to Sun Valley to ski with ski school director, Sigi Engl. It was the winter of 1949/50 and I was already traveling and showing my first feature-length ski film to any group of two or more people that would sit still to watch it.

Back in Washington, D.C., President Truman assumed that while the Shah was skiing, someone might try to assassinate him. The Shah had brought sixteen bodyguards with him from Iran but none of them could ski, so the head of the ski patrol asked for volunteers who could handle a .45-caliber automatic pistol.

Four patrolmen seemed like the right number of men to handle the job. The designated four were issued army surplus automatic pistols and told to drive out to Warm Springs and practice firing a half dozen magazines, adjust their shoulder holsters, and be ready to ski the next morning.

Everything worked to perfection. Two of the patrolmen were skiing in front of the Shah and Sigi, while the other two skied behind them. After a few days of skiing like this, everyone at Sun Valley got used to the group and the guards began to relax.

The Shah was a powerful skier, hurtling down almost any slope in a very wide snowplow. He had learned to ski on his own ski lift near Teheran and particularly enjoyed skiing in the moonlight. When Pat Rogers heard about this, he arranged to have a party at the Roundhouse two-thirds of the way up the side of Mt. Baldy. After an evening of dancing, caviar, fine champagne, and a full moon, the party got into their ski gear and, with torch lights blazing, skied down the canyon.

Those who couldn't handle night skiing got to ride down on the Exhibition lift; it was there that the first hint of trouble emerged. Having had too much champagne at high altitude, a man on the lift hollered at the man riding down in front of him to throw him the half-full bottle of champagne to ward off the chill of the midnight moon.

Turning around in a single chair and throwing a bottle of champagne on a fifty-foot upward slant is no mean task. The bottle flew through the air but was about two feet short of the catcher, who, as he reached out to grab it, fell off the chair.

Halfway down Exhibition, a half-drunk Iranian who couldn't speak English was now stuck knee-deep in snow. By the time the ski patrol left the Roundhouse with a toboggan and got the drunk to the ambulance at the bottom of the hill, the sky was turning gray in the east. Had the Iranian not been so full of champagne, the evening might have turned out tragically.

The next day, during lunch in the Roundhouse, the ski patrolmen hung up their automatic weapons on the clothes rack, covered them with their ski patrol parkas, and went over to the cafeteria counter to order lunch.

Watching all of this, a friend of mine said,

94

"Why don't we switch parkas with them, take theirs and two of their guns, and see what'll happen."

I walked over with him and stood directly in the line of sight between the parkas, the guns and the Sigi, the Shah, and his guards. While I stood there, the instigator of this potential international incident switched our two, sort-of-the-same-color, red, parkas for theirs and draped them over two of the automatic pistols. He handed a parka and a gun to me and we sauntered casually out the door, climbed into our skis, and skied quickly down Canyon and River Run.

At the bottom, we left the guns and holsters hanging on a fence, covered them with the ski patrol parkas, and told the lift operators to keep their eyes open for Sigi, the Shah, and the four ski patrolmen later in the day.

The two patrolmen who couldn't find their guns wisely decided to just fake it for the rest of the day. Sigi and the Shah never did know that the firepower of their guards had been cut in half, and skied the rest of the afternoon in the Christmas Bowl. When they got to the bottom of the River Run lift on the final run of the day, the lift operator hollered at the group as they skied by. One of the ski-patrol-guards-without-guns skied over and was very embarrassed when he was handed the two guns and parkas we had "borrowed" at lunch.

I couldn't help but wonder what today's ever-present media would have had to say if a drunk had fallen off a chairlift or a prank with guns had been played during the Clinton's learn-to-ski vacation. Somehow, I think that our journalists would have raised these incidents to the level of a national crisis, and Janet Reno would have ordered a multi-million dollar investigation.

"Warren, you are an orthopedic surgeon's annuity."

THE NEEDLE

I have decided that there are two types of people in the world today: those who have bad back problems, and those who can tell you how to fix your bad back problems.

Unfortunately, I belong to group #1, rather than group #2. I originally hurt my back when I was playing basketball in college and have tried just about every supposed cure known to man: chiropractors, acupuncture, kinesiology, massage therapy, exercise, hard beds, soft beds, yoga, swimming, rolfing, and even ignoring it.

I haven't tried orthopedic surgery, spinal fusion, or titanium rods inserted in the vertebrae. Mostly, because I'm too much of a coward.

But my back still hurts most of the time.

Recently, after not sleeping for a month, my wife Laurie finally dragged me, kicking and screaming while riding lying down in the car, to an orthopedic surgeon in Seattle.

On the way to Seattle from our island, Laurie and I were taking our early morning walk on the upper deck of the ferryboat, when I had an omen drop right out of the sky. A seagull that had been on a fairly steady diet of battery acid mixed with rancid fish entrails hit me right on top of the head with his morning constitutional. I managed to wipe it off the top of my head but, by the time I got it cleaned off the shoulder of my jacket, it had eaten a hole in it so big that my jacket was now an off-the-shoulder model.

I won't tell you what I said to Laurie for laughing so hard at my predicament.

Three days later, after all kinds of tests and finally armed with a couple of dozen x-rays, an MRI, and drugged up with half a dozen pain pills, I met with the designated orthopedic surgeon for the first time.

His nurse had me climb into the mini-muumuu that you tie in the back. I hadn't even been able to tie my shoes for a month, so there was no way I was going to be able to tie the smock in the back. My wife had to do it for me.

With all the x-ray photos of the inside of my body spread out before the orthopedic surgeon, his first words to me were,

"This is great Warren. You are an orthopedic surgeon's annuity. Now I can get those braces put on my kids' teeth and maybe even enroll them in private school."

This was the first time in my life that all of those insurance premiums didn't sound like such a bad monthly deal to me.

I had to have him repeat a couple of times what he was going to do to my aching back to make it well. When he outlined the same operating procedure twice, I knew that I was really going to be stuck.

"My plan is to inject a mixture of steroids and anesthetics inside your vertebrae. I do this by simply laying you on your stomach and threading the length of the ten-inch-long needle through the various vertebrae until we get to the top of the problem. However, in your case we might also have to inject the needle from above because we might not be able to get it in far enough from below."

I suggested that,

"I could get the shot from below and stand on

my head for an hour a day and maybe the medicine would drain in that direction."

"It doesn't work that way," he replied, with a gleam in his eye that looked as though he had already endorsed my first check to his kids' orthodontist.

"Warren, all you have to do is step into the x-ray room and lie down on your stomach, and we can get this over with in a few minutes."

I muttered, "Yeah, we can do that as long as I know the x-ray room is soundproof, you strap me to the table, and then give me a silver bullet to bite on."

He dragged me down the hall, where I met his assistant who apparently had overslept because he was still in his green pajamas and wearing a shower cap. His assistant mumbled something I couldn't understand because he was mumbling it through a green facemask. I never did understand why he needed a shower cap.

Then, with about as much enthusiasm as a snowboarder after lunch on his first day of learning, I waved goodbye to my wife and entered the dreaded, leaded, combination x-ray and torture room.

If you ever want to hear a grown man scream and cry, just show him a ten-inch needle with a half-gallon syringe on the other end of it. If you want to hear him really holler, all the doctor has to say is,

"We're having trouble getting the needle in as far up your spine as we need it to go, so I think I will just try a little more pressure."

That didn't work either.

Fortunately, I never heard him say,

"Oops!"

But he did say,

"Sorry, I can't make it go any farther, so it looks like I'll have to insert the needle back up near your shoulder blades and come down from above. I hate to have to do this to you, but it has to be done."

"It won't hurt much."

I learned years ago that, when a doctor says it won't hurt much, hurt is a relative thing. The needle does not go into the doctor, but into some part of MY body that has to then be followed up with a lot of stitches or a cast to correct a mistake I made while trying to act thirty years younger than I really am.

Half an hour later, I was wringing wet with sweat and trying to get out of my mini-muumuu and listen to what the doctor was saying about how good my back was going to feel in a week or two.

"And if it doesn't feel better by then, come on back and I will see if I can place the needle a little more strategically next time."

Now I know why Mother Nature gave the job of having babies to women. There would be no future generations if it were up to men.

THE QUICK-CHANGE ARTIST

This morning I had to go to my bank at the ski resort town near where I live and see about yet another bank loan. That meeting required a fairly formal dress code; then I had to go to a book-signing fundraiser at that same resort. I had to wear my ski clothes for that because it gets very cold sitting outside all afternoon, answering questions and signing books.

I spent most of the first forty years of my life changing into my bathing suit in the front seat of cars when I went surfing, so it wasn't a big deal for me to change into my ski clothes in the bank parking lot. I was sitting there between meetings, changing into my ski clothes, when it happened.

I had taken off my shoes, socks, and pants and was about to put on my long underwear when a car pulled up and parked alongside of me. Sitting there in my jockey shorts, I paused in my change of clothes for the lady who was driving to get out of her car and walk into the bank.

As she walked by my side of the car, she glanced in at me sitting there in my jockey shorts and screamed at her young daughter, "Lock the car doors, there's a pervert in that car. I'll run inside and call 911. You keep hollering pervert."

I barely had time to get my long johns on and wrestle my snowsuit up as far as my knees when there was a bang on the side door and I was looking at one the ski resort's finest cops. The red lights were flashing on the roof of his patrol car and his partner was talking over the PA system, "O.K. out of the car with your hands over your head."

I was now standing in the parking lot with my hands over my head, with my freshly cleaned snow-suit down around my ankles soaking up the melted snow and mud.

"You look just like that guy that makes the ski movies."

"I am."

"I don't think so. In the movies, he drives a different kind of car and would have his skis and boots with him. You don't have any ski gear with you."

"Put your hands on the roof of the car and spread your feet apart."

Spreading your feet apart with your pants down around your bare feet while standing in the mud and snow is not an easy thing to do, especially on a clear, cold Colorado morning in a ski resort in front of a gathering crowd.

The daughter of the lady who originally screamed "pervert," was now out of her car, pointing at me and hollering, "pervert, pervert" just as her mother has taught her to do.

I was finally allowed time to explain to the officer why I was half-naked in my car in the bank parking lot. It was then that he recognized my voice from some of my videos that his kid played endlessly.

This defused the situation a little.

About that time, another patrol car came roaring into the parking lot with sirens howling. Out jumped another officer and with him was the biggest snarling dog I had ever seen - the local K-9 drug-sniffer-patrol.

Whenever there is a chance of an unusual arrest at this ski resort, the drug patrol is required to respond. By now, I had talked the arresting officer into letting me pull my snowsuit up out of the mud and get more fully dressed. I was then ordered to walk around to the back of the van and open the doors. The 120-pound, snarling German shepherd leaped inside and began to sniff around for any drugs in the six boxes of books I had for the book signing. He quickly went almost berserk with his barking. When he did that, the officer guarding me told me to get in his police car while the other officer continued the drug search.

It was then that I remembered that I hadn't cleaned out the van from our last book-signing trip. The trip where my wife, Laurie, fell in love with yet another cat at the pound. En route home from Idaho where she bought the cat, she had spilled some cat food and catnip in the back of our van and this is what the dog had found. He was now reacting as though I was smuggling ten kilos of marijuana in the back of my van.

About this time, my wife came out of the crowd that had gathered to watch the drug bust. She had the president of the bank with her. They were both giggling as they vouched for me. Laurie told the police that I had never even smoked a regular ciga- rette in my entire life, nor had a drink of alcohol, much less done drugs of any kind.

By now, the original officer on the scene was sitting in the patrol car with me and asked for my autograph for his snowboarding kid who wanted to get in one of my movies. He also apologized and said, "Any time our K-9 smells drugs, the sergeant on duty has to come to the scene and sign off on the gathered evidence."

There were five patrol cars now surrounding my van, along with six officers and a K-9 dog. One of the officers had about nine ounces of Kitty Delight in a plastic bag that would be held as evidence until my case eventually came to trial.

They let my wife and me go on to our book signing at the base of the ski lift under our own recognizance. Before they let us go, the sergeant told me, "Better clean out your van and be a little more careful where you change your clothes next time. In the meantime, you have to sign this ticket for indecent exposure. This is not an admission of guilt and anything you say can be held against you in a court of law."

The first thing I did when I got home was to phone a company that tints car windows. For a little extra, I found out they can put on a double coat so no one can see into your car. Then I got my ski suit cleaned. Perhaps my days as a quick-change artist should be over!

THE TRIP TO LALA LAND

The other day I got on an airplane and, as usual, fell asleep before it took off. And, just as Gulliver did in his travels, I woke up in a land of make believe.

Los Angeles - where your first experience is trying to find the carousel that is supposed to have your baggage from your mythical flight. I was once again introduced to the law of the airport. "It will take as long for your baggage to get from the airplane to the carousel as it did to get your body from where you left to where you arrived." A note here: my wife always packs for these short trips as though she is going to dinner with the Queen of England at Buckingham Palace and then skiing in St. Moritz for a week. This was a four-day business trip, but my wife is famous for the line, "Just in case".

The trip from the curb to the car-rental garage was in a bus big enough to hold the entire Super Bowl football team and driven by a lady who was about four-foot-eleven, weighing ninety-four pounds, and had just graduated from the Race Driving School in San Francisco. Fortunately, they had seat belts on the bus or we would have wound up in a heap, just like the baggage did against the front windshield when the bus got cut off by a speeding automobile being chased by a police car.

The rental car pick-up went without a hitch, except the rental clerk had to have someone standing by him translating everything I said into Spanish so he could enter it into the computer.   As I crept towards the on-ramp of the freeway to merge with the evening rush-hour traffic, I realized that I had not done this for a few years. Perhaps that is why the butterflies in my stomach were bigger than in the stomach of a third-day skier when he discovers he is committed to making the second turn on a black diamond, mogul-filled run. Fortunately, the off ramp was closed for repairs, so I doubled back and drove on the surface streets for what seemed like an hour and a half.

I finally found another on ramp and this time it was, "Set the course for Santa Barbara, no matter what." Once into the mainstream of the evening traffic, I watched as car after car changed lanes and slipped into the space between my car and the one in front of me. A rule of Los Angeles freeway driving is, "If there is enough space between you and the car in front of you for another car, another car will cut in front of you and fill it up." By the time we got over Sepulveda Pass and got ready to handle the interchange to head for Santa Barbara, I was tailgating just like Dale Ernhart in the Winston 500 and going about as fast. We had to drive the seventy-five miles to Santa Barbara in a little under an hour and never even got in the fast lane.

A late-night snack, a motel, a good night's sleep, and things were better. The next morning was the kind I remembered as a child in California. You could see forever, and the sun was sparkling off the glassy water in the harbor full of sailboats. The oil drilling rigs stood stark against the horizon. As Laurie and I walked out on the breakwater, we saw a bearded man sitting in the sun drinking his morning cup of coffee. He had a large ring in his nose and a heavy silver chain hanging from it that was attached to his right earring. Not too unusual for the beach cities, but in his case it was in sharp contrast to his green-and-gold dyed hair that hung down to his shoulders. He did have it braided in a rather darling manner, however.

As we turned around to head back to the motel and our meeting, I was almost knocked down by a couple on roller blades, both in a deep crouch and racing towards the acquisition of total body fitness. The were dressed in matching black and purple spandex tights, silver-booted roller blades with alternate green and red elbow pads (some sort of port and starboard designation, I imagine), gold knee pads, and red brain buckets. The second person was drafting the first, just as I had been drafted in my car while driving to Santa Barbara. Except all the second person got to see was the fanny of the person in front of him while they were crouched down and working out.

Our business meeting went very well and we avoided a lot of the freeway on the way back to LALA land by taking the coast route. The only major difference was that the ocean was on our right all the way back to Santa Monica, but the cars were driven just as fast and there was no center divider, so I really stayed out of the fast lane.

We were scheduled to spend four days in a seminar and were guests of an old friend. The first morning I took the wrong route to the seminar and was held up by a freight train that was twice as long as most chair lifts I ride in the winter. It was also moving at about one third the speed of a chair lift. As a result, I was thirty minutes late to the first morning of this seminar for getting things done on time. Time management, I think they called it.

I had enrolled in it because I never seem to have enough time to get stuff done. Right now I am involved in the following: collecting bicycles to ship to third-world countries; getting two salmon streams recreated in the northwest; writing the script for my next feature-length film; trying to complete my autobiography by October of 1999; getting ready to publish another collection of my newspaper columns; setting the time aside to go to a Mammoth Mountain College fund raiser; and ski five or six days a week for at least three or four hours. Not to mention supervising getting our boat ready to go to Alaska next summer.

And I showed up late for the first day of a time management seminar.

If I had only taken the freeway instead of the side streets to get there, I wouldn't have met the freight train. However, I might have gotten swept into the middle lane and wound up back in Santa Barbara, or maybe Palm Springs before I ran out of gas in my compact rental car.

On the noon break, I hurriedly glanced through a copy of the Los Angeles Times. I like to read the funnies and then the rest of the paper but, in this case, the ads ARE the funny paper. Here are a few of the ads I noted: Nose blocked? Call 1-800 735 FACE; Hair transplants, only $4.98 per graft, no minimum required; Laser face rejuvenation; Not all Fen-Fen programs are created equal; Medical weight loss; Sculpture your body with Laser surgery… By the time I had skimmed through the paper, I knew that Southern California was indeed the land of the remodel.

Let's see: at $4.98 per hair graft, I would have to spend $13,946.98 for that; Liposuction for my stomach would be $11,374, because they do it by the pound of fat extracted; my wife needs a pager so she can get all of her phone calls, so that's $74.95 per

112

month for the rest of our lives; two pairs of roller blades and matching spandex outfits with arm and knee guards will cost us $745.99; and a Frontal Lobotomy is $93,000. That last one is so I can eliminate my acquired-with-age knowledge so that I could match the fourteen-year-old kid my wife thinks I act like.

All of this is why I left LALA land for the mountains.

I'm too old to remodel!

"I'm too old to remodel."

"El Nino hadn't been invented in 1965. But I always found plenty of unusual winter weather. In Zurs, Austria, there was always lots of powder snow. On my left is Herbert Jochum, owner of the Hotel Lorunser, who was featured in many of my films from 1955 through 1970."

BLAME IT ON EL NINO

I pulled up my two crab traps and found that I had a limit of six good-sized crabs to clean and take to dinner at my friend Richard and his wife's house. When we got to his home on another island, he was busy impressing a guest with his golfing ability by trying to drive a golf ball into a small boat that he has anchored off his beach.

My wife went into the kitchen to start cooking the crabs; a few minutes later she came out and said, "There's a golf ball rolling down the lawn behind the house."

Richard had whacked a three-wood against a tree and it had ricocheted and landed about seventy yards behind us.

I gave him eleven years to ever be able to do it again and he said, "Next time El Nino is here, I'll be able to do it again."

It seems as though everyone is blaming El Nino for anything that goes wrong with his or her life.

A recent news bulletin from Moscow stated that the life of their Space Station has been shortened by at least ten years because of the radiation effects of El Nino.

The spin-doctors in the White House are creating a story that will tie the cold weather of Washington last winter to the fact that President Clinton had no alternative but to succumb to the advances of Monica Lewinsky. They are going further out on a spin-trip by stating that El Nino has already altered the DNA of whatever is on the now-famous dress. As a result, it will not be admissible as evidence in a court of law.

Those same spin-doctors have now blamed the crisis in the Middle East on El Nino when, in reality, the Middle East was used as an excuse to get President Clinton's midlife crisis off the front page.

Almost a month of over 100-degree temperatures in Texas has destroyed over ninety percent of their crops. As a result of El Nino, of course! In the 1930's, they had the same drought in the Midwest, which created the Dust Bowl. The farmers put everything they owned in the back of their cars and drove to California and started over. I think there was an EL Nino in 1935, but no one knew what to blame the unusual weather on back then.

Our golf course here on the island gets a lot of rain during most of the year. As a result, we play by winter rules, which lets you move the ball out of the mud or the rivulets that sometimes come over the top of our gumboots with cleats. The last three weeks have been very hot and dry and the golf course has turned from lush, green grass to asphalt-hard brown dirt and yellow grass. When you hit a drive, the ball rolls down the fairway sideways to where the creek normally is, which is almost as far as I drive it. So, now we play by El Nino rules. This means that we get to move the ball halfway back up the side of the hill to where it hit the ground the first time, before it started rolling sideways for two or three hundred feet.

We recently met an old friend who has put on an extra 41 pounds in the last six months. Naturally, she blames it on El Nino.

Recently there has been a major outbreak of E.Coli 0157:H7 in a variety of places, ranging from hamburgers and coleslaw to a spring that is the water supply for Alpine, Wyoming. Before medical detectives got hot on the trail of the latest outbreak in Wyoming and a water park in Georgia, some publications were blaming El Nino for the mutation of E.Coli. It is usually one of the most beneficial bacteria in the body and metabolizes food in the intestines.

But, back to our dinner.

Our host Richard forgot to turn over the halibut on the barbecue. The smoking halibut turned out to be about the same color and texture as the asphalt driveway at the golf course. Fortunately, his wife Nancy had some lamb in the freezer that she immediately put on the barbecue while it was still frozen. Meanwhile, I brought up the little-known fact that Dolly, the cloned sheep, would not have be alive today if it were not for El Nino.

The lamb was cooked perfectly on the outside but still raw on the inside. The medical detectives say, "Do not eat partially-cooked meat." Laurie and I decided to make our dinner grilled-cheese sandwiches when we got home.

When we got there, the lights in our house didn't work because there had been a five-hour power outage on our island. Instead, we each had a bowl of melted ice cream by flashlight and began to wonder what else we could blame on El Nino. Personally, I hope El Nino stays around for a long time, so that I'll always have a scapegoat for my lurching disasters!

A portion of the 8,743 people who saw Warren's 1960 ski film in St. Paul, Minnesota. Tickets were $1.50 each, unless you stopped in Schuneman's Department Store and bought something in their ski shop worth $5.00 or more. If you did that, you got two 50% discount tickets.

DISCOUNT TICKETS

Almost everyone I know today has to spend too much time shopping for airfare deals. At the same time, Untried Airlines employs over five hundred men and women in one building somewhere on the planet. Their only job is to keep track of mileage-plus members and the tens of thousands of supposedly free tickets that they earn every time anyone pays a hidden surtax for each airline ticket they buy. Or they spend one dollar on their credit card to get some kind of mileage award towards one free mile of airline travel.

Let's see now. If I pay for my new Mercedes Benz 500 SL with my Untried Airlines affinity credit card, I can get a free round-trip ticket from Los Angels to Las Vegas, provided I fly between the hours of 12:01 a.m. and 5:15 a.m., except on weekends. Otherwise, it will take two Mercedes Benz purchases with the same credit card to fly at a decent time of the day.

When Early-American Airlines first invented mileage plus, they didn't have a place to fly people, that was a desirable location for a one-week holiday. Some wise executive decided to apply for a flight from Los Angeles to Maui. Now, every day of the week, Early-American Airlines flies a DC-10 round-trip to Maui, and as many as 95% of the people on the plane are flying on their mileage-plus awards for free.

It doesn't take much of a mathematician to figure out that whenever you pay to fly, you are contributing your overhead to support that entire free mileage-plus ticket overhead. That, or else the airlines are losing money on purpose every time anyone flies free.

Probably one of the few benefits of being a senior citizen is that I can buy discount airline tickets and am supposed to be able to fly between any two cities in the United States, except Alaska and Hawaii, for $140 each way. I can fly all the way from Seattle to San Juan Puerto Rico, for $140.

When I tried to get my senior citizen discount airline ticket for my flight from Seattle to Denver and back the other day, I discovered there was probably only one seat on each flight at that low rate. Of course, that seat was sold to the grandmother of the person in flight reservations three-and-a-half months ago. What I didn't know was that, regardless of age, I could fly round-trip coach on Monday and Tuesday from Seattle to Denver for only $960.

Why do I have to pay $960 to sit alongside someone who only paid $140 to ride for two hours each way? And he is a Sumo wrestler who weighs twice as much as I do.

I think I will go to Las Lenas, Argentina, instead, and ski for a week for only $35 more. That $995 includes airfare, hotel, meals, and lift tickets on a hill that has eight ski lifts and four thousand vertical feet of skiing.

However, if I still want to go to Denver, if I fly out of Seattle at 6:00am and fly back at midnight, I can do it for only $520. If I could make my last-minute emergency business reservation two weeks in advance and leave Seattle at 6:02am and return the next day at 12:01am, I could do it for $280 round-trip. Of course, I would have to stay over a Saturday night and rent the right kind of car and stay in an officially-approved hotel in a room next to the elevator shaft.

What would happen if ski resorts sold their lift tickets the same way.

Let's see...

"It is a powder snow day so let's charge twice as much." We very seldom hear, "It's a little icy in the center of the trails today, so let's offer a 13% discount."

If you live in a house with an even-numbered zip code, that will entitle you to a $14.72 discount on even-number days of the month. If you lived in an apartment on an odd-numbered floor in an odd-numbered zip code, you would be entitled to a $14.73 discount. In order to be eligible for this discount, all you will need is a certified copy of your birth certificate, your social-security number, and your drivers license, to prove where you live, and that you are who you look like you are. If you don't have any of the above, just ask for the discount anyway and they will accept your AAA card.

The two scenarios about airline fares and lift-ticket prices are about as absurd.

Some ski resorts today really have almost 150 different lift-ticket prices and for the same resorts, the $48 lift-ticket price averages about $34 on an annual basis. Why not lower the face value of the ticket to $39? Then the resort could eliminate all of the money they spend on printing, advertising, and distribution of the coupons at the rental-car agencies, supermarket, and gas stations, as well as buying all the ads in newspapers at nearby, competing ski resorts.

Why does someone who doesn't know any better have to pay $48 for an all-day lift-ticket so he or she can sit alongside three teenagers who are chewing tobacco and spitting it into the snow, while riding on the same chair, and they only paid $48 for a season pass? That's because their high school is in the right zip code.

Why not eliminate the hundreds of different discount rates and just lower the basic cost of a lift ticket to $39? The resort would net $5 more per ticket on the average than they are doing today and the skiing public would be ecstatic with the price reduction. The only disadvantage to that is a lot of people would start skiing again and the lift lines would get longer.

But back to the current problem at hand of my airplane seat since the ski lifts are closed for the season. Closed, in spite of record snowfalls during the month of April and so far into May.

They used to have ten or fifteen discount seats on each flight prior to the inaugural flight to the International Baggage Mangling landing field in Colorado. Now they only have one discount seat on each flight to help pay for the cost of building the new International Airport. Or is it to pay for the $210,000,000 per year that Untried Airlines pays for your luxurious waiting room that you can wait in when your flight is late. Except that the chairs are all bolted to the floor and you can't put two of them together to sleep. Which you will have to do when there is two feet of snow outside and your flight has been canceled for the next fourteen hours.

Maybe if I bought a six-pack of Mercedes automobiles on my affinity credit card, I could make a reservation for a free ticket to my next emergency business meeting. This meeting would be when they issued a warrant for my arrest for insufficient float on my credit card and obtaining automobiles under false pretenses. My preliminary hearing to answer charges would be held on September 23rd in Broken Spoke, Nebraska. Broken Spoke doesn't have an airport that you can fly to from anywhere else. That is, unless you charter a single-engine airplane that can land on a grass field, or choose to ride a Greyhound bus.

The bus passes through Broken Spoke at 3:17 am and the nearby CatchAll Motel is listed in the AAA travel guide as "cash or money order only, NO personal checks whatsoever, some rooms with showers, morally clean, luggage required."

So, my question is how old do you have to be to retire and not have to take any business flights?

Or, better yet, where should I move to, so I can get the best discounts on my lift tickets next winter?

"I had a hard time finding the right length ladder so I could reach all of the shredded garbage that the rotary snow-plow had deposited in the trees in front of our house."

WHAT GOES AROUND
COMES AROUND

What goes around comes around, and rotary snowplows have the habit of always doing it at the wrong time in my life.

In 1947, when Ward Baker and I were living in an eight-foot trailer in the Sun Valley parking lot, we figured that we would only be there a few days before we were told to move on, so we simply buried the first five or six days worth of our trash and garbage in the snow bank behind the trailer. We intended to dig it up on the first bad-weather ski day and haul it over to the trash heap.

The next Monday morning when we were cooking an early breakfast of oatmeal and frozen milk, the hotel detective came by and asked us if we would move our car and trailer so they could plow out the parking lot. The car battery, of course, was dead by this time (it had not gotten above seven below zero since we parked the car), so the company wrecker had to tow our rig out of the way. When the rotary snowplow came roaring and blasting its way through our parking spot, it sprayed milk cartons, frozen rabbit carcasses, a frozen loaf of bread we had misplaced, and all other manner of used and unused trash up into the trees behind our camping spot.

The hotel detective took a rather cavalier attitude about the new parking lot decorations and said,

"Well at least your friends can now find your trailer more easily."

125

And so for the rest of the winter, we told people, "We are camping under the aspen tree with the faded milk carton and the back half of a frozen rabbit hanging on a couple of limbs about fifteen feet above the ground. And when the sun is right, just about twenty minutes before sundown, it will reflect off the bottom of the Campbell's soup can with the label dangling and blowing gently in the evening breeze."

As I said, what goes around comes around and rotary snowplows have the habit of always doing it at the wrong time in my life.

All through November and December, the road in front of our winter home in Vail has been getting a little narrower with each new dump of snow. We have been able to get past another car going in the opposite direction only when one car or the other car dodged into someone's driveway. Some of our neighbors have someone show up and plow out their driveways after each snowfall. Other owners actually have shoveled all of the over-two hundred inches of snow that has fallen since before Thanksgiving.

We live at the end of a winding road and it is always hard to describe exactly where our house is located because we're partially hidden behind a beautiful stand of tall snow-covered pine trees.

Monday is trash day in our neighborhood and the first Monday of the month is also when the rotary snowplow is available to widen our street back to its full two-lane summer width.

In the wee hours of last Monday morning our house finally became very easy to find because that rotary snowplow roared right through our three trash barrels, as well as a half dozen white plastic garbage bags full of Holiday debris. They were instantly shredded and then the seventy-nine pounds of frozen "confetti" was plastered all over our snow-covered yard, our trees, and everything else within forty feet of the now-wider road.

Monday dawned as a crystal-clear, below-zero day that was just perfect for skiing. Just eight inches of new, light, powder on top of fourteen perfectly groomed runs that I was scheduled to show our houseguests.

Instead, I wandered around our front yard for two hours in my never-before-used-snowshoes, picking up bits and pieces of pulverized trash. It is amazing how much trash you can put in a single plastic bag when it is shredded and blown all over an area approximately the size of two basketball courts. It is even more amazing how long it takes to pick up each scrap of it when the snow that was blown from the bank beside the road to land on top of them already buries about fifty-four percent of them. Until the middle of the afternoon, most of our snow-covered trees looked like a kindergarten class had made all of their Christmas decorations out of old milk cartons, frozen orange peels, some canceled checks, and a six-pack of banana skins.

When I finally got around to picking the shredded debris off the trees, it was a real challenge to find the right length ladder. I finally found one under the back porch that was holding a cord of wood up off the ground so it would be dry when we put it in the fireplace. Just to get there, I had to dig a seventy-five foot path from the street through four feet of snow. Once I moved the cord of wood and dragged the ladder out to the road, I had to dig a hole down through the waist-deep snow to the ground alongside the first tree full of trash. Then, I had to place the ladder on the frozen ground so it wouldn't slip out from under me. Finally, I needed to climb up high enough so I could try to knock the milk carton remains out of the outstretched tree limbs without knocking the rest of the snow on the upper limbs down onto my head.

I spent thirty minutes trying to figure out how to step out of my now slightly-used snowshoes and onto the fourth rung of the ladder without slipping and falling into snow up to my waist.

It is obvious that I failed this basic test of Mountain House Maintenance but at least I didn't have to wax my skis on Monday.

By the time I got all of this figured out and about 38% of the trash recovered, it was an hour or so beyond my normal time to eat lunch. I was warming up in the dining room and had my peanut butter and jam sandwich about one-third eaten when the phone rang. It was my neighbor Wolfgang wife, Betty Lou, who lives a few houses down the street. Betty Lou was complaining about how much she disliked my wife and me living in the neighborhood because they had to explain to their house guests that the neighborhood didn't always look quite this trashy.

And, here, I thought I had just managed to avoid lurching into a near-disaster by not falling off the ladder!

FRANCHISED FOOD

I can remember when the dinner of choice on any restaurant menu was steak, medium rare, a baked potato with lots of butter, bacon bits and sour cream, maybe some spinach or carrots on the side, and a chocolate sundae for desert.

That, of course, was before the invention of fat calories, cholesterol, and the importation of exotic dishes from all over the world.

In many American cities today, you can dine on Korean, Taiwanese, Japanese, or Chinese food, to mention just a few. I know that people who live in those countries have less heart trouble than Americans do; on the other hand, there are no Oriental players in the NBA.

The other day, my wife took me to an off-the-beaten-path Vietnamese restaurant in Wailuku, Maui, where she suggested that I make my choice between #19, BAHN HOI GA NJONG TOI, or #16, which was BAHN HOI CHEY, or perhaps #37, which was BAHN HOI CHA GIO.

It had taken me a dozen years of skiing and filming in Europe to finally learn the difference between SCHNITZEL ALA HOLSTEIN and STRUDEL MIT SCHLOG. Now Laurie expected me to be able to decipher Vietnamese at first glance.

She tried a little of her Vietnamese language skills that she learned when she was a stewardess flying the wounded back from Vietnam, when the waiter replied in very proper Oxford English,

"We have an English-language menu if you

prefer. It describes all 217 different dishes that our chef can prepare for you in seven minutes."

All of the numbered dishes my wife had already suggested were the equivalent of Vietnamese Burritos.

Instead of hamburger, chili sauce, onion, cheese, and all of the good fat-building stuff in a Mexican Burrito, here is what BAHN HOI contained: basil, mint leaves, cucumber slices, lettuce, bean sprouts, vermicelli rice vermicelli, radishes, and pickled carrots.

The various sub-categories, such as GA NJONG TOI, CHAY, or NEM NUONG were the different main ingredients in the burritos.

Number nineteen was grilled and sliced chicken breasts, #6 was a vegetarian burrito with TOFU. Now there is a real nothing! What tofu is, I don't know, except that it tastes and looks like cup of custard without anything sweet in it to make it edible. You can have tofu baked, boiled, broiled, or you can pass it up, which is what I always do. It goes down a little like Jell-O, or about the same as opening your mouth and running into the wind.

NEM NUONG turned out to be barbecued-pork meatballs. I never have been able to barbecue meatballs without them eventually falling apart and becoming part of the charcoal briquettes themselves. If you buy cheap meat for your meatballs when you barbecue them, that extra grease makes the flames a lot hotter.

BOI LUI is beef sirloin-rolls.

I opted for #19 and Laurie opted for #6.

Now comes the do-it-yourself, build-your-own Burrito trick.

They supply you with a couple of six-packs of what looks like tortillas, a plate full of garden vegetables about five inches high, and numerous small dishes full of lethal-looking sauces. All of this, along with the largest finger bowl I have ever seen.

I really had to depend on my wife for guidance.

The tortillas were so thin they were almost transparent. When Laurie told me they were made out of rice flour, it made no sense to me. I used to build kites with rice paper in the Boy Scouts, but I never tried eating the rice paper that I made them out of.

She picked up a transparent Vietnamese Tortilla and slid it into the large bowl of hot water. The hot water softens them up so you can now move them over to a plate and start filling them up with whatever you unknowingly ordered. That is, if you know how to use chopsticks.

I watched with fascination, as my wife wrapped a complete dinner salad up into a transparent piece of flexible rice paper, added some broiled tofu, and then dipped it into a sauce of some kind. She ate it like a Popsicle that she had just dropped into a pile of grass clippings, and she did it all with finesse, except for the one bean sprout about two feet long that had gotten hung up in her pile of sliced cucumbers and mint leaves. She looked like she had an intravenous feeding-tube stuck in her mouth.

This is when you find out where the phrase, "Love is Blind," came from.

Now it was my turn, and after the fourth or fifth Vietnamese Burrito, I was beginning to like them. This was about the same time as the big bowl of hot water had cooled to the air-conditioned room temperature and it no longer made the transparent rice "paper" soft enough so you could roll up what was left of your salad.

I eventually ate the last three sheets of stiff

rice "paper" that I had glued together with my leftover grated peanuts, mint leaves, a last slice of cucumber, four bean sprouts, a vermicelli cake noodle, and some pickled carrots.

After we both ate a six-pack of Vietnamese Burritos, I paid the $39.43 luncheon bill, tax and tip included, and headed for the car, wondering why I was still hungry. I felt "appetite neglected" and fortunately there was a Burger King in the next block. There, I easily and quickly disposed of a Burger King with cheese, a large order of fries, and washed it all down with a large chocolate shake.

I did all of this as I contemplated franchising the Vietnamese restaurant I had just left.

McDonalds was laughed at when it first started, and I have been laughed at for some of my ideas as well.

But I need a slogan for my new restaurant chain. Somehow I don't think there will be a big market for it, if I simply call them what they are.

Vietnamese Burritos.

BAND AIDS AND HORSES

Many years ago, when I was romancing my wife, I decided that a good vacation for us to take would be a pack trip somewhere. However, I had to spend almost every day all winter long with a rucksack full of cameras on my back, so hiking with a rucksack was out of the question. During a phone call to my old friend Syd Cook in Sun Valley, he offered us the last two places on his horseback riding/pack trip in the Bob Marshall wilderness in Montana. It was coming up in three weeks.

I made the mistake of saying, "Why not?"

Syd and his wife Mary were so far into the horse-riding way of life that they have their own barns, horse trailers, and trainers for their horses that danced for fun and games.

Dressage, I think they call it.

Three weeks later, we met them after a routine one-mechanical delay, two lost-bags, and a three-different-commuter-flight trip to somewhere in Montana. This was followed by an uncomfortable but predictable four-hour ride standing up in the back of a truck that was normally used to haul cattle to the slaughterhouse. We were going to meet the guide and the horses we would ride.

We arrived at the corral just before midnight, after traveling for sixteen hours from Southern California. There, we were handed two sleeping bags, two foam pads that were so thin they would be called sheets anywhere else, and a tent to pitch if we wanted to stay out of the rain.

Which happened to be occurring at that precise moment.

Two hours later, I finally had our tent pitched and was arranging the foam pads, when Laurie had that "I wonder how I got myself into this" look in her eyes.

Very few hours later, after throwing rocks out from under my sleeping bag at deer that kept hanging around the tent and eating what grass there was, there was a loud banging and clanging and someone hollering, "breakfast."

The cattle truck had already left, so we had to stay and ride the horses. At breakfast we were told that our destination was on the other side of the Continental Divide at a ranch, 120 miles away. We had six full days to make the trip. This would be over a 12,000-foot pass and roughly the same distance as riding by horse from Denver International Airport to Vail.

Which, in retrospect, was really dumb, even if your are deeply in love with your saddle partner.

By noon of the first day, my fanny reminded me that it had been at least 45 years since I had ridden a horse.

Here's a typical day in the life of a reluctant cowboy.

The wrangler/cook, the guy who's in charge of the horses, the mules, and helps with the meals, would wake us up before six in the morning. There were twelve people on the trip, so everybody had to first coordinate the use of the outhouse tent. After that, my job was to roll up our sleeping bags, then the paper-thin foam sleeping pads, and take down and roll up our tent, while Laurie rolled up our clothes and packed them in our rucksacks. This, of course, was after she put Band-Aids on my saddle sores. And I had a couple of real doozers. My Jockey shorts had seams in exactly the wrong places for sitting in a saddle all day. Somehow, I knew that if our budding romance could survive fanny-doctoring the first thing every morning, that there had to be a very bright future for us.

Several of the people on the trip were avid hikers, so they would walk while we rode. Which, when you are paying $100 a day or more for the use of a horse, a tent, and three meals, not using the horse seems kind of dumb.

By the time we got to the Continental Divide, we were into the routine of packing and bitching, and bitching and unpacking, while looking forward to doing something different from sitting in a saddle all day and wincing with each step of the horse.

On the downhill side of the Continental Divide, a whole new set of blisters began to appear, so I got to stand up in the stirrups for hours on end. That, or cry like a baby for the same length of time.

On the fourth day, I was helping load up the mules with the packs since the wrangler looked like he could use a little help, when he told me that he worked seven days a week moving whiners like me back and forth on the same trail. His day usually started at four in the morning and ended about ten at night. For all of this work, he was earning almost $70 a week.

In his words, "I'm lucky to have the job. I get my food, I get to sleep under the stars, and there are a hundred guys waiting in line to take my job if I ever quit."

On the afternoon of the fifth day, for some reason we didn't have to ride so far and hard. After lunch, I decided to go fishing and the camp dog followed me as we walked about a mile up a side-stream. I was catching and releasing fish with almost every cast and "Old Yellow" had wandered off upstream. I was fighting that once-in-a-lifetime, big one in a deep pool, when I heard him barking and then yelping and whining as he headed in my direction. I had only one thought; "He's rousted a bear." He came running down the bank of that stream like a cut cat dipped in turpentine. I thought, "Oh, Oh! Here comes the bear. The dog will hide behind me, and all I have to defend myself is this skinny fishing pole."

Old Yellow ran right by me without even slowing down.

I don't know if that bear ever showed up at the fishing hole because I beat Old Yellow back into the camp by thirty seconds and hid between the dinner table and the woodpile, back in the far corner of the cook tent.

That night, I found out that our wrangler/guide was part Indian and in an after-dinner ceremony, I was given my official Shoshone Indian name *"Very-Old,-Yellow,-no hair,-many-Band-Aids. "*

I can live with the name. One thing I can't live with is the thought of another pack trip.

WHAT'S THE DUMBEST THING YOU EVER DID?

After the fund-raising race last weekend, a bunch of us wound up at the local Chinese restaurant. A meal there is a good deal because they have big round tables and a lazy Susan in the middle. Because of that, anyone can order anything they want, everyone else gets a taste of it, and you get a taste of everyone else's order. After having a plate full of almond duck, peapods, steamed rice, fried rice, wontons, bong fu duck, beef teriyaki, lettuce, tacos, volcano shrimp, and endless swallows of tea from a cup the size of a small thimble, it was time for the fortune cookies.

With a pause in the conversations, someone asked everyone around the table to tell about the dumbest thing they had ever done. I waited awhile and listened to everyone else tell his or her dumb story. I would be hard-pressed to figure out the dumbest thing that I have ever done, because I have done so many of them.

The stories that were told should be repeated here. One man told of how, when he was a kid in Canada, he and his pals used to steal candles and then go down in the sewer and light them and see how far they could walk before the candles burned out. It was hard to walk because they had to crouch down. At the same time, they had to walk with their feet three feet apart so they would be partway up on the round sides of the sewer pipe instead of just wading in the muck. It wasn't until the fourth sewer expedition that they figured out that if only one person burned their candle at a time, they could navigate underground from one end of the city to the other.

A pillar in the community told us that one time he was in Spain where, after lunch he was taken out to see a ranch where they raised and trained bulls for the ring. After watching a couple of young bulls and apprentice toreadors, the owner of the ranch asked him, "Why don't you try it?" Being from Texas, he immediately said, "Sure, why not?"

After a few minutes of instruction, he was standing in the center of the ring and they let the bull loose. Fortunately, there was someone else in the ring to attract the bull because our friend didn't quite understand the concept until his instructor once again said, "You hold the red cape out to the side, not directly in front of yourself."

Another one of the Chinese food aficionados volunteered that his dumbest trick was when he was playing high school football. Practicing during the summer was very hot, so after practice he steered the entire high school football team to a hotel on Sunset Blvd that had a king-size swimming pool. Once there, 34 crew cut, muscular, football players proceeded to drop their drawers and dive into the pool in the buff. For some reason, some of the paying guests took offense at this and called the police. Our Chinese food friend who was telling the story was the captain of the football team and so the police arrested him and hauled him away to jail. His folks were out of town, his brother had to borrow some bail money from an aunt, he missed the next two football practices, and the team's in-the-buff, midnight-swim almost cost him his professional football career before he even graduated from high school. Luckily, this same man, not to be named here, didn't do any other dumb, politically incorrect things, because he ended up very high in Republican politics.

Then another man told of driving a stream-lined racecar at 740 miles-per-hour. That's right, 740 mph! At that speed, you could drive from Vail to Los Angeles in about an hour and fifteen minutes. You might miss a curve or two, but that's all the elapsed time it would take. Imagine a car without tires, instead, with wheels made of aluminum. At 9,000 revolutions per minute, there is no rubber compound known to man that would not disintegrate. He described this journey at that rate of speed as if it was no big deal. You just climb into the vehicle, fire up the turbine, and it takes sixteen seconds to go from a dead stop to 740 mph. At twelve seconds into the journey, while he was subjected to six times the pull of gravity, he got to ignite a sidewinder missile that was attached somewhere for the final thrust to get him up to the top speed. He thought he went 742 mph but when all of the measurements were in, he had only gone 740 mph. My question of course was, "What does two miles-per-hour difference mean at that rate of speed?" And just as dumb a question was, "How do they measure something that accurately?"

There was no doubt about it from the people who were by then munching on the cold remains of Chinese food. We all voted him the winner of doing the dumbest thing of anyone at the table, without a doubt.

He won, hands down, even after they got me talking about some of the dumb stuff I've done such as: windsurfing from Maui to Molokai; skiing on an active volcano that was blowing up every day between 3:30 and 4pm; flying in a three-place heli-copter after dark with five people, four pairs of skis, and over a hundred pounds of camera gear; riding down on the roof of an aerial tram in France that is over a thousand feet above the ground; producing three or four hundred ski movies in the last fifty years and helping to create long ski-lift lines around the world.

Lift lines that I always wind up standing at the end of.

Then we all opened our fortune cookies and I think I won that one because mine said, "You would look better with a crew cut."

THE EAGLE HAS LANDED

My wife Laurie and I were leaving the next day for Alaska.

This would be no cruise-ship tour with moonlight dancing on the deck while gliding by glaciers with seven hundred senior citizens aboard and the potential of polyester poisoning hanging heavy in the air.

We were going in our own boat.

That's right. After a decade spent cruising the waters of the Northwest in a variety of boats, we finally have topped out on three-foot fever. (That's when, no matter what size boat you have, you always want one that is three feet longer.)

Our first boat was a twenty-footer in which Laurie and I went on trips for as long as six weeks. After a couple of years of cruising with a Coleman stove for cooking, a Coleman lantern for heat, a Gatorade jug for fresh water, a porta-potty, and an outboard motor, she finally decided that she wanted a boat with a genuine shower and a flush toilet, so we opted for a 28-footer. This had all of the luxuries anyone could want; however, even though we are the best of friends, living in about 150-square feet for a month or so at a time got a little crowded.

The boat had a top speed of 47 mph, but we still almost died in it when we got sucked backwards into a gigantic whirlpool in Big Bay, Canada.

But that is another story.

Four and a half years ago, we borrowed a lot of money and went for greatness.

We contracted with a major manufacturer of sport fishing boats in New Jersey. Pacemaker had built 14,000 boats since 1947, and we expected delivery in June of 1992. Pacemaker went bankrupt one boat before ours. We own the last Pacemaker ever built. When we finally retrieved the hull after fighting the bankruptcy court and the bank over it, we had it trucked out to Anacortes, Washington, to be finished by Cap Sante Marine.

But that's another story too.

Boating is like standing in fifty pounds of ice cubes under an ice cold shower and tearing up hundred dollar bills.

In our new boat, we were able to tear up hundred dollar bills in the cozy warmth of an enclosed flying bridge while watching whales and eagles play as we leisurely made our way north to Petersburg, Alaska. While fishing for salmon, digging for clams, and gathering oysters, we could worry about red tides and currents that in places are 20 knots on the chart at full flood tide.

Going this far north was a first for both of us.

There was no definite departure date and no definite return date. All we asked was that the charts for our navigation are up-to-date. Just as important, I hoped that I had somehow learned enough to: keep two 400 HP diesel engines running properly, along with a water-maker, radar, depth sounder, GPS, Chartnav, VHF radio call signals, cellular phone and fax, a twelve-KW generator, several different fishing rods, reels, and down-riggers, the proper mixture for the outboard for the dinghy, what you can and cannot take through customs, rules-of-the-road so we wouldn't run into a tug towing a barge or the cable in between them, how to walk in the woods full of brown bears without a rifle, and how to have a good time so that the next time we don't have to go to Alaska on a cruise ship and run the risk of polyester poisoning.

A couple of the things that I insisted on when designing our boat was that I have a computer station, a printer, and a modem to send my columns back to the newspapers on a weekly basis.

Investigation revealed that for $9,000, I could purchase a satellite telephone that would send faxes and I could phone from anywhere in the world. The only trouble is that it costs $2.50 a minute to use, plus a connection fee of $5 per call. I opted instead for a cellular phone and I can always stop along the way at a Marina and use their fax machine for $2 or $3 and deliver the columns that way.

The afternoon before we departed set the tone for our upcoming adventure.

There was a seagull sitting on the end of our dock while I was installing the Dole Fin on my inflatable's outboard. The seagull got dive-bombed by an eagle and frightened into flight. The eagle chased it for a minute or two until it was grabbed in mid-flight. At the same time, a pair of crows were making a lot of noise and harassing the eagle. Having badly wounded the seagull, the eagle then dropped it in the water and hovered low over it until the seagull drowned.

When the seagull finally went limp, the eagle retrieved it and flew away with it to its nest on a nearby island to feed fresh ice-cold seagull to its newly hatched children.

And Laurie and I haven't even left the dock yet!

"It was as if I'd won the $10,000,000.00 sweepstakes the day I bought my first camera at the age of nine. I've been living on the interest of that investment ever since."

SUPER BOWL MANIA

Not everyone can go to the Super Bowl, but the next obvious question was asked last night after a dinner party. We were all sitting around the fireplace discussing snow conditions when Agnes said, "I can't go to the Super Bowl because I got a registered letter today from Ed McMahan that said I was the winner of ten million dollars. To get the prize, all I had to do was be sure to be home when they drove up to my house on Super Bowl Sunday with the check."

Agnes is a college graduate and I assume she is very smart, so when she was questioned further, she did admit that she had read the fine print. It stated, not very clearly, that she would have a better chance of being the final ten-million-dollar-recipient if she just subscribed to one more magazine. All she had to do was call a semi-toll-free, 900 number and let the operator know if she would be home or not on Super Bowl Sunday. Ed McMahan doesn't like to go on a blind date and get stood up. It doesn't make for good entertainment if he and the entire TV crew come knocking on your door and you are off in San Diego at the Super Bowl and all they have for TV coverage of the big winner is an unanswered door bell. What will they do with the oversized check, the balloons, and the bottle of champagne?

Agnes called the semi-toll-free, 900 number and was very surprised that she got an answering machine. She told the machine that she had already subscribed to 43 magazines to survive the yearlong trip to the finals. She already was having a hard time reading at least a magazine-and-a-half a day so that when the 43 new magazines come every month, some of last month's magazines were still be unread.

She had subscribed to everything: Martha Stewart, Popular Mechanics, Time, Newsweek, Ladies Home Journal, and would subscribe to the National Enquirer if Ed McMahan offered it. When the Ed McMahan sound-alike voice called her back, he first made an offer to buy the two Super Bowl tickets she had and then convinced her to stay at home. After all, she had survived a year of magazine subscription mania and was one of fewer than a hundred finalists in the state of Colorado.

That phone caller had such a smooth voice that he could have sold Agnes the pink slip for the Gondola at Vail.

During the sales pitch for that one last magazine subscription, Agnes tried to explain that she had call forwarding on her cellular phone. Wouldn't that be enough so that if they phoned her at the game, she knew she could get cellular reception in the football stadium in San Diego and she would make sure her phone was turned on?

This lady has a problem. She can watch the Super Bowl from the comfort of her living room couch, answer the door when the bell rings, and be ten million dollars richer, and all she has to do is get one more magazine a month in the mail.

Instead, she will drive for two-and-half hours to the Denver Airport and then fly to San Diego. There, she will spend three days partying while getting ready to watch eleven men who have a total body weight of 2753 pounds try to beat the brains out of eleven other men who have a combined body weight of 2785 pounds.

However, she and her husband are good friends of the coach of one of the teams that will be playing in San Diego, so she doesn't want to disappoint him. At the same time she doesn't want to disappoint Ed McMahan when he drives up to the house.

Now she has a real problem. There were nine people in the living room at the time this discussion took place. It was easy to tell which ones had also phoned and gotten the same answering-machine message. They too were finalists and had already made up their minds to stay home and get the ten million dollars. They were all encouraging Agnes to go to the Super Bowl. If Agnes went, that would get rid of one more potential winner and they then stood an even better chance of being the ten million-dollar-winner.

I was one of the people who told her to go to San Diego. I also have some unread copies of Wood Worker's Monthly, Building Log Homes for Fun and Profit, and Extreme Knitting for the Non-athletic.

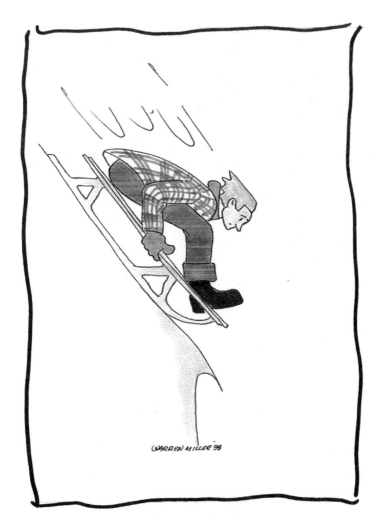

"In Southern California in the late 1930's, I never went up to play in the snow in the local mountains until after Christmas."

PRE-SEASON SKIING

The ski lifts at Alta, Utah were built in 1938, because a very peculiar atmospheric and geological phenomenon always makes the snow fall in Little Cottonwood Canyon by mid-November. By the early 1950's, die-hard skiers with fat wallets would fly all the way to Salt lake City, just to get some early skiing over Thanksgiving weekend at Alta.

In those days, Alta only had two chairlifts that hauled almost four hundred people an hour. A chairlift line never developed because there were very few people skiing that early in the year. (Or later in the year for that matter.)

About that same time, Dave McCoy, with his two rope tows above nine thousand feet at Mammoth Mountain, was offering the same early-season ski experience. This was also due to the unique atmospheric and geological phenomenon. Mammoth, however, was a seven or eight hour, 350-mile-drive each way, on a narrow two-lane road from Los Angeles. Even with that huge population center, there were still no early-season lift lines.

According to the calendar, the official start of winter is not until December 21st, the longest night, or the shortest day of the year.

When I was a Boy Scout in Southern California in the late 1930's, we never went to the local mountains to play in the snow until after Christmas, but three out of five years there was enough snow for sledding during Christmas vacation. Then when I found out about skiing and girls, I quit the Boy Scouts and have been skiing ever since.

Today, any resort with deep-enough pockets tries to get its lifts running before Halloween, or at the latest, Thanksgiving. Massive amounts of water, money, huge electric bills, million-dollar snow making machines, cloud-seeding, native-American rain dancers, and dozens of high-priced ecological attorneys try desperately to cover hills with a form of frozen water that the director of marketing calls man-made snow. This is done as soon as the temperature gets below freezing for at least one hour a day. Nowadays, snowmaking machines are as loud as the noise of half a dozen jet airplanes taking off at the same time.

What this early-November, ski-resort-start-up-madness really accomplishes is to let the new employees figure out with whom and where they will be living, as well as what they will be doing all winter. For example: Rad Brad and his three fraternity brothers from Northwestern have a job working nights at the local Pizza parlor. They all have graduate degrees in marketing and they get minimum hourly wages, mileage for their 1973-Ford Falcon and any leftover pizzas when they go off shift. They also get all day off to ride their boards with semi-free lift tickets until the real season kicks in, the week of Christmas/New Years. Since there is only five inches of snow on November 17th and a lot of rocks that are six inches high, the runs can't be packed with the $275,000 grooming machines.

The resort management knows that Brad and his buddies will pack it down between most of the rocks. In the process of body and snowboard packing, management will give the new employees at the hospital plenty of practical experience mending breaks, and sewing up the worst cuts and abrasions. This rush of minor accidents also gives the new secretaries at the closest hospital a few extra weeks to learn the computer programs for quicker coordination between the insurance claims and the payments. With luck, Brad will tweak a shoulder just enough so he can get workmen's comp for the winter and still be able to ride his board all day, every day. By then, he will be rooming with Steve Stunning, the out-of-work lifeguard who is collecting his unemployment insurance for the winter because his swimming pool in Syracuse is closed until May 15th. Steve doesn't ride a snowboard because the clothes aren't fashionable enough. He got ski clothes free for modeling at the discount ski shop's fall fashion show in Buffalo in September.

The pre-season fry-cooks are trying to learn how to make pancakes that at least taste better than cornmeal pizza with no topping.

In November, on chairlift number seventeen, old Pop Eberhardt is teaching the new lift loaders how to hold the chair so it will hit you in the back of the leg with maximum velocity just before you load, so you don't have time to say anything. If they slip the chair under you just right, you will drop at least one piece of your equipment while you are still wincing from getting on the chair. By spring, the "You lost it, we found it" department at chair number nineteen will have 214 right- handed gloves, 83 pairs of broken goggles, 311 left mittens, and two cell phones labeled, 'demo only, not for sale' in their stash.

The new ski patrol persons are learning how to shovel snow, ski at the speed of an Olympic downhill racer while hauling a broken body in a toboggan, and doing CPR and mouth-to-mouth resuscitation while trying not to start any early-season romances.

151

Grace Hootenberger has been chosen to be the mouth-to-mouth patient because she is so homely she could make a train run on a dirt road.

November is when the highway snowplow operators warm up their huge snowplows and practice racing over the passes while the steel blade makes pretty sparks in the early evening on the warm, dry asphalt. By the time there is enough snow to plow off the road, they will be skilled enough at angling the blade so that they will be able to deflect the snow and rocks into the windshield and hood of every car that tries to pass them.

November is also when the many ski and snowboard publications switch into high gear. They are sending their February issue to the printers and they only have one more issue to create this winter. All of the people who work in editorial can now spend the winter skiing free everywhere, while working on articles that they tell the host resort will be published and distributed next August in a magazine that has a November date on the cover.

November is when the old timers know that when the snow level is down to ten thousand feet, in about thirty days it will be down to where they have to shovel it out of their driveway. They also know that in April there will be eleven feet of snow under the chairlift at Agony Acres, bright sunshine, T-shirt weather, and they will have the whole hill almost to themselves. It's what we call pre-season, pre-season skiing!

A WHALE OF A TALE

Over the years there have been a lot of remarkable achievements on skis. Last winter, the mythical 150mph barrier was broken. In 1968, Killy won three gold medals in the Olympics, a feat that has never since been duplicated. Howard Head invented the metal ski almost 50 years ago. Twenty years ago, Jake Burton invented the snowboard. In the heart of all of us is the Walter Mitty reality that if only we had done something a little different we, too, would have some sort of immortality. We could have become a Picabo Street, a Scott Schmidt, maybe a Dave McCoy or a Pete Seibert.

Many of us have achieved some sort of personal athletic goal that is a great accomplishment, but only in our own minds, goals such as: breaking the stairstep record at the athletic club; climbing to the top of Vail mountain in less time than anyone else we know; or riding a bike from Vail to Aspen over dirt trails. Yes, these are all records of sacrifice, dedication, training, or singleness of purpose. But, do they show valiance?

We had some guests the other day from Australia and took them to the Whale Museum on a nearby island where I saw an exhibit recording the ultimate achievement in any athletic endeavor that I have ever heard of.

During the spring and summer, the gray whales travel north to the Arctic Circle to feed on the abundance of sea life that live and breed there. In the fall when the whales head south to the waters of

Lahaina, they travel along the coast before heading further west. The Indians who lived on the coast during the past millennium had an entire village depend on the killing of one or two of these 80-ton monsters to survive the harsh winter of big storms, of rain and snow.

They didn't have Gore-Tex clothes to wear or thermo-pane glass in their long houses. Their clothes were made of pounded and woven cedar bark and probably were a lot itchier than anything you can imagine. They were expert in catching salmon on lines of deer sinew or twisted cedar-bark with just the right-shaped piece of bone carved into a rough-shaped hook. After many sacrificial ceremonies, when there was a lull in between storms, the toughest guys in the tribe would paddle their long boats out into the straits and ocean when they heard the whales coming. In the silence of calm weather, you could hear a whale surfacing a mile or two away.

Positioning themselves in the whale's path, they had sealskins in their boats that somehow had been sewn into bags that would hold air. The object was that one of the long boats would be able to stick a small harpoon into that 70-ton whale, throw the airtight-skin balloon attached to a long line over the side, and follow the 60-foot-long whale with the floating skin attached, as the whale kept right on swimming, unmindful of the small pin-prick of a harpoon.

The paddlers had their work cut out for them. They had to paddle as fast as the whale would normally swim so that, when it surfaced, they would be there to stick another small harpoon into it. Again, with a small float of yet another skin attached. (I still can't figure out how they tanned the hide, sewed it up, made an airtight bag out of it, and then someone in the boat blew it up while they continued paddling.)

Keep in mind, this entire exercise was for their survival of the winter.

It might be raining hard, the air temperature about 40 degrees, and the ocean temperature between 42 and 48 degrees. The paddlers were sweating, trying to keep up with the whale. (It's no wonder that whales head for the warm waters of Lahaina, Maui.)

The long boats have about 20 or 30 of these harpoons with inflatable skins stuck into the whale, which is starting to have a hard time swimming. It might even be rolling over occasionally to rid itself of these nuisances so it can get on with its journey to warmer water.

Now the critical moment is almost at hand. The most macho of all of the men in the long boat is about to perform his ultimate athletic feat. It makes three gold medals look like child's play; riding a bike to the top of Vail Pass in 15 minutes would be easy for this guy.

The whale has given up and the paddlers who have been at this for three or four hours are exhausted. But the whale's lungs will fill up with water and he will sink unless Hushtah, with a large needle in hand, and about 200 feet of sinew, does his job quickly and expertly.

His job is to dive overboard in that 45 or 46 degree water and swim underwater to sew the whale's mouth shut before he sinks. I would guess that 15 or 20 feet of needlepoint on a whale's lips might take at least half an hour. Anyone I know would die of hypothermia in ten minutes trying to swim in water that cold.

Once the whale's lips were sewn shut, Hushtah climbed back into the long boat, and, with the other eleven men, tied a strong line around the tail of the whale and towed it five or six miles back to the beach in front of the village. There, they might have to wait for high tide so they could get it as close as possible to the long house. Then when the tide went out, they could start cutting up their winter's groceries.

And they did all of this in itchy, cedar-bark clothes.

Yes, the whale-lip-sewer-upper gets my vote for being the most macho man I have ever heard of, accomplishing an Olympic feat.

Hushtah, from the Northwest Coast Salish Indians, swam after the whale in forty-five degree water, while wearing a skirt made of itchy cedar bark.

YOUR TAX DOLLARS AT WORK

I was tallying up my expenses for our book-signing, speech-making, road trip in a Salt Lake City motel when I read that Bill Clinton was bringing Chelsea and Hillary to Deer Valley for a learn-to-ski weekend.

It had to be a cosmic occurrence of some kind for us, because Laurie and I were scheduled to do a book signing in nearby Park City during this same weekend. We were resuming our fund-raising efforts for the Steadman-Hawkins Research Foundation. The Hawk had done a good job of repeatedly putting me back on my skis. I stupidly tore my left rotator cuff in September while trying to get in shape for skiing by doing push-ups. (Five years ago, The Hawk fixed my right shoulder and, had he not performed that surgery, my skiing days would have ended forever in the spring of 1993.) After skiing for sixty years, it is now my turn to put something back and the Steadman-Hawkins Research Foundation is one of the several research projects I really believe in.

But back to the presidential family and their first learn-to-ski weekend.

According to all accounts, it turned out to be the most expensive ski weekend in history.

Beginning with the expenses of transportation for the First Family from Washington, DC, to Stanford University in Palo Alto, California, to pick up Chelsea, to Park City, Utah, to LA and back to Salt Lake City, then back to Stanford to drop off Chelsea, and then back to Washington DC, for the final helicopter flight back to the White House, follow these expenses:

Air Force One has a fixed daily operating overhead of $37,000 - not including mileage. They arrived in Deer Valley on Thursday, so, except for a quick Democrat Party fund-raising trip to Los Angeles on Saturday for Bill, the plane was parked from Thursday until Sunday night (that's four days at $37,000 a day). There is also an Air Force Two that flies everywhere Air Force One flies, as a decoy or in case Air Force one runs off the runway or the bedrooms are all occupied. That's another $37,000 a day. According to the newspaper accounts, this $37,000 a day per plane does not include the cost per mile to fly each of the 747's. Nor does it include the entourage of soldiers who guard the plane 24-hours-a-day when it is parked, technicians who stay on board to keep in touch with the goings-on around the world, or the three shifts of secret-service men with ear plugs and concealed weapons to guard the first family. Also not included in the bill is ten learn-to-ski weeks to enable the security guards to ski in front of and behind Chelsea and Hillary down the beginner's slopes. Those learn-to-ski weeks came in at about $1200 per security guard (ten times $1200 is another $12,000 to add to the bill.)

Reportedly, there were 136 people in the White House family's entourage that descended on Deer Valley.

To transport the first family and the various guards, cooks, servants, and people to put skis on and off, from the Salt Lake airport to Deer Valley, required the flying of eight bullet-and-bombproof vehicles. They were flown from Washington on a C-147 cargo plane that probably cost as much as Air Force One, or an additional $37,000 per day, plus mileage.

The ski weekend consisted of Hillary and Chelsea doing a little traversing and kick-turning on a ski slope where no one else was allowed, while Bill sat and relaxed in a friend's house. The press reported that he read his latest fan mail and tried to somehow calculate the number of e-mail-circulated jokes that have been created about him in the last couple of months because of his reported activities.

While we sold my latest book on the plaza of the ski resort at Park City, anyone who had not been cleared by the CIA and the FBI was asked to leave downtown Park City. This forced the closing of about half the retail shops. I don't know what their loss of revenue cost them! While Bill's wife and daughter traversed and kick-turned, he was chauffeured downtown from Deer Valley. There, he had a cup of coffee while the TV cameras and press took advantage of his "pressing the flesh" of potential Utah voters, as they call it in newspaper talk.

While all of this was going on, there was a small band of Utah Republicans who were keeping track of what the weekend was costing taxpayers. When they added up the expenses of the staff and Air Force One, Air Force Two, and the C-147 for four days, with around-the-clock security guards to protect it from souvenir hunters, the final tally for the ski weekend was reported to be $3,700,000. (That's three million, seven hundred thousand dollars.) About the same price as the six-bedroom house they were staying in free as a tax-deductible item for the owner.

We paid a lot of taxes on our book-selling, fund-raising trip just to help the First Family enjoy the Deer Valley ski weekend.

I guess the First Family's trip put all of Our Tax Dollars To Work - and then some!

SCHEDULE OF SHOWS

SCHEDULE FOR WARREN MILLER'S "MANY MOODS OF SKIING" 1961/62

OCTOBER
15—Reno, Nevada (State Building)
16—Ogden, Utah (Ogden High School)
18—Salt Lake City, Utah (Highland H. School)
19—Denver, Colorado (Phipps Theatre)
20—Denver, Colorado (Phipps Theatre)
21—Boulder, Colorado (Macky Theatre)
22—Denver, Colorado (Phipps Theatre)
23—Denver, Colorado (Phipps Theatre)
24—Colorado Springs, Colorado (City Aud.)
25—Spokane, Washington (Shadle Park H. S.)
26—Wenatchee, Wash. (Wenatchee Val. Jr. Col.)
27—Vancouver, B.C., Canada (Queen Eliz. Thr.)
28—Sleep on Greyhound Bus
29—Bend, Oregon (High School Auditorium)
30—Eugene, Oregon (Roosevelt High School)

NOVEMBER
2—Tacoma, Washington (Jayson Lee Jr. H. S.)
3—Seattle, Washington (Palomar Theatre)
4—Seattle, Washington (Palomar Theatre)
5—Seattle, Washington (Palomar Theatre)
6—Portland, Oregon (Benson High School)
7—Portland, Oregon (Benson High School)
8-13—Los Angeles, Calif. (Wilshire Ebell Thr.)
14—Sacramento, Calif. (Sac. City Col. Aud.)
15—San Francisco, California (Nourse Theatre)
16—San Francisco, California (Nourse Theatre)
17—San Diego, California (Hoover H. S. Aud.)
18—St. Paul, Minnesota (St. Paul Aud. Arena)
19—Syracuse, New York (Regent Theatre)
20—Buffalo, New York (Amherst Theatre)
21—Ann Arbor, Michigan (Ann Arbor H. S.)
22—Detroit, Michigan (Ford Auditorium)
23—Toronto, Ontario, Canada (Massey Hall)
24—Toronto, Ontario, Canada (Massey Hall)
25—Cleveland, Ohio (WHK Studio One)
26—Lynn, Mass. (City Hall)
27—Providence, R.I. (R.I. Schl. of Design Aud.)
28—Worcester, Mass. (Burncoat Jr. H. S.)
29—Cambridge, Mass. (Cambridge H. S.)
30—Andover, Mass. (Andover Memorial Aud.)

DECEMBER
1—Hartford, Conn. (Bushnell Theatre)
2—Schenectady, New York (Niskatuna School)
3—Hanover, New Hampshire (Webster Hall)
4—Garden City, New York (Garden City H. S.)
5—Baltimore, Maryland (Towson H. S. Aud.)
6—New York City, New York (Hunter College)

7—Philadelphia, Pennsylvania (Town Hall)
8—Teaneck, New Jersey (Teaneck High School)
9—Pittsburgh, Penn. (Sol. & Slrs. Mem. Aud.)
10—Burlington, Vermont (Burlington Aud.)
11—Grand Rapids, Michigan (South H. S. Aud.)
12—Madison, Wisconsin (West High School)
13—Duluth, Minnesota (High School Aud.)
14—Green Bay, Wis. (West High School Aud.)
15—Wilmetter, Illinois (Howard School)
16—Oak Park, Illinois (High School Aud.)
28—Sun Valley, Idaho (Opera House)
29—Sun Valley, Idaho (Opera House)

JANUARY
4—Yuba City, California (Yuba College)
5—Santa Barbara, Calif. (Santa Barbara H. S.)
6—Los Angeles, California (Poulson Hall)
8—Redding, California (Redding High School)
10—Santa Ana, California (Santa Ana H. S.)
11—Hermosa Beach, Calif. (Pier Ave. Aud.)
12—San Gabriel, California (Mission Playhouse)
15—Palo Alto, Calif. (Palo Alto High School)
16—Palo Alto, Calif. (Palo Alto High School)
17—Palo Alto, Calif. (Palo Alto High Schoo)
18—Ontario, Calif. (Chaffey H. S. Aud.)
19—Whittier, California (Whittier High School)
20—Midland, Michigan (Central Intermediate)
22—Rochester, New York (Chamber of Com.)
23—Montreal, Canada (West Hill High School)
24—Montreal, Canada (West Hill High School)
25—Montreal, Canada (West Hill High School)
26—Mt. Tremblant, Quebec, Can. (Mt. Tr. Ld.)
27—Rutland, Vermont (Rutland H. S. Aud.)
28—Sleep aboard the Vermont Central
      Amalgamated R.R.
29—Keene, New Hamp. (Keene Jr. H. S. Aud.)
30—Wilmington, Vermont (Mt. Snow Lodge)
31—Pittsfield, Massachusetts (Berkshire Mus.)

FEBRUARY
1—Sleep aboard 707
2—Portland, Maine (Portland High School)
5—New London, New Hamp. (Colby Jr. Col.)
6—Manchester, New Hamp. (Pract'l Arts Aud.)
7—Waterbury, Conn. (Wilby H. S. Aud.)
8—Milwaukee, Wis. (Shorewood Theatre)
9—Port Huron, Michigan (High School Aud.)
15—Aspen, Colorado (Opera House)
17—Taos, New Mexico (Lodge)
18—Mayo Clinic (Rochester, N.Y.)

DROP YOUR FRIENDS A NOTE AND TELL THEM WHEN WE'LL BE IN THEIR CITY WITH OUR SHOW

"With a schedule like this for almost forty years, I was a large part of my travel agents retirement plans."

WINEMAKING IS AS ART

It had taken me seven months of tough negotiations to finally land a contract to produce a docu-
mentary film about one of Northern California's lead-
ing wineries. The winery was just north of the world-
famous Napa Valley and had been producing fine
wines in the same building there for over a hundred
years. It was a rare two-story winery that was built
before the electric pump became available, and in
their case, before electricity. A railroad went right by,
alongside of the ancient stone building; some of the
local folklore about their great wine was that "the
daily shaking of the ground when the trains rumbled
by made for a better fermenting process."

The winery's owners lived in England and the
distributor was located in New York City near the
Staten Island Ferry. Their advertising agency was
located a $15-taxi ride away, at the other end of
Manhattan.

These negotiations occurred before the invention of fax machines, Fed-Ex, videocassettes, E-
mail, or all of the other timesaving inventions that
make business decisions so much easier today.

The only way we could expedite any ship-
ments would be for me to take my script revisions to
the airport ticket counter and send it to the airport in
New York. The client would then have to send a $40-
messenger out to La Guardia to pick them up.

Billing me, of course.

Countless script revisions went back and forth
via this method of counter-to-counter delivery. When

I finally had it refined and in enough detail to what the client and the advertising agency thought would sell wine at their tastings, a meeting was scheduled and we got together at the winery in Northern California. I had to show them exactly what I had in mind in the way of images and how the documentary/advertising film process would work.

There are some critical things in the creation of a bottle of wine that had to be scheduled very far in advance.

For example: when the sugar acid ratios of the grapes have matured to just exactly the right amount, the contract pickers send their workers into the fields and the grapes are picked and crushed, whether our camera crews are there or not.

We had to film the bottling room, but we couldn't be working in there while they were actually filling the bottles. The vintner thought that we might contaminate the wine as it was going into the bottles.

Have you ever seen "tasted" wine before it has a chance to get into a bottle and become drinkable? I still don't know how the vintner can tell when the crushed grapes are ready to bottle. In the big, open, 10,000-gallon oak barrels, it looks a little like a stagnant pond that should be full of mosquitoes and pollywogs. No one could ever explain to me what it was supposed to look or taste like during the three months we had our camera crew working there. I know it sure did look terrible.

During the get-ready portion of film making, the client and advertising agency account executive had time and time again made minor corrections in the script. Every scene and every word of dialogue, as well as recorded sounds, had been very meticulously orchestrated and committed to print.

However, what appeared as neat little words

typed on a piece of white paper with black ink, couldn't begin to convey the feelings of this hundred-year-old building and some of the employees who had worked there for over fifty years

I had the utmost confidence in my production crew's ability to deliver the film the client thought he wanted and not stray too far from the script they had approved.

We toured the fields and talked with the manager about his best estimate on when the grapes would be ready to pick, transport, and crush. This was to be the theme of the movie, *From Grapes to Glass*. We had to follow and film the entire wine making process. We walked the fields from dawn to dusk deciding on when the sun would be at just the right angle for the best pictures.

Once we finally had the exterior shots figured out, we moved inside to film the shining glass beakers in the laboratory of the vintner, the oak barrels, the ten-thousand gallon stainless steel tanks. I also wanted to get close-ups of all of the old timers, the dozens of different people who create the glass of wine you might enjoy in five or ten years.

We watched them sulfur the barrels, making new barrels and repairing old ones. I was trying to acquire knowledge rapidly enough to stay ahead of any idea changes that the client and the advertising agency account executive might want.

A nagging question kept coming back to me: how do they know if they are doing something exactly right so, at some as yet unspecified distant time, a glass of wine from that small oak barrel or ten-thousand gallon stainless steel tank will taste just right for your celebration? Capturing the process of wine making on film would be like trying to make a ski movie exciting if everybody's skis were nailed to a porch.

"Cue the Grape Vine."

"O.K. Action. Start growing."

The four of us, the client, the account executive, and my cameraman/director, were wandering through the barrel room on the third afternoon, when I started talking to a man who had worked at the same job for sixty-three years. He was sulfuring the barrels. This is part of the wine making process where they burn a small amount of sulfur in the barrel to kill any bacteria that might be left from the last vintage.

He started telling me some stories of old-time wine making when he was a lot younger.

"I was sulfuring the barrels one afternoon when I heard someone holler,

'Silencio!'

"Everyone stopped what they were doing when they saw the new vintner with his ear pressed against the bung of a barrel of cabernet."

"He's listening to the wine!"

"He explained to us that this was his way of telling if the process of fermenting was on time and on cue, and that it depended on all of his senses - taste, smell, and sound."

The man telling the story had a great, weathered face and a fantastic storytelling voice.

I turned to the client and said, "So much for our detailed script. There is the film and the title for it - the faces and the voices of the people who create the wine." "From Grape to Glass."

I mentally tore up the meticulously prepared script right on the spot. It was a wrap! Winemaking *is* an art.

TOTAL RECALL

When the ski resorts start shutting down in direct ratio to their location north of the equator and their altitude above sea level, I head for the ocean. There, I have spent a good part of my life riding surfboards, racing sailboats, somehow surviving on windsurfers, and driving powerboats.

I have always had a sign on my boat that says, "Everything that is known about boats has already been written. All you have to do is read all of it, have instant total recall and you will never get into trouble."

I've read a lot of boating stories, but it is the details of how they got out of the trouble I'm in, while I'm in the middle of the same troubles, when total recall most often escapes me.

I have had a lot of experience in racing small sailboats. I began racing catamarans in 1962. I often single-handed my Olympic Tornado catamaran to Catalina for long weekends. I wore a wet suit and took a sleeping bag, Primus stove, and some backpacking food in a garbage bag hung from the boom. All of this and a gallon of water too. I have also raced long distance races in my Hobie-33 ultra-light keelboat, and finished third in the World Championships in Sydney, Australia, in my J-24. (We finished third with my son Kurt driving the boat. I handled the spinnaker and brought the credit card). Since that time, my sailing has been limited to windsurfing; when they say, "The wind is free," it is.

What costs a lot of money is the place to store your equipment.

Several years ago, I towed my twenty-foot camera boat to the Northwest and found out there was another side to boating. What came into focus for me about any kind of boating is, "It's not the doin', it's the learnin'."

Most often, the learning is a little painful, very expensive or both.

The first three years of cruising southern British Columbia with my wife in my twenty-foot outboard motorboat, there was no way to have total recall because I couldn't find anything written about how to do it. People thought we were just plain crazy to cruise in a boat with only a single outboard motor, a cutty cabin, a Coleman stove, an ice chest, a Coleman lantern for heat, a porta-potty, a bunch of charts, fishing tackle, a crab pot, and a lot of luck.

We didn't know you should have a spare outboard motor, a radio, depth sounder, radar, or other stuff like that. After all, we would never be out of sight of land during the almost five hundred miles we cruised that first summer. Besides, we wouldn't have known how to use anything electronic anyway.

But after three years of moving things around on what we now call "the little boat," my wife wanted running water, a shower, and a genuine flush toilet. So, we chartered a 28-footer the fourth year and in the fifth year we bought a Florida-built boat, a 28-foot Regal with what I thought was a roll bar.

It turned out to be an arch to mount radar on.

Webster defines "recall' as the ability to remember something. Remembering it at the right time is the critical element in the process of staying out of trouble in a boat.

For example:

I learned, while cruising in my 28-foot Florida-built boat with the radar arch/roll bar, that there is a great patented gadget that you can buy instead of expensive davits for mounting a dinghy on the swim step of any yacht under fifty feet long. It works like a charm, but it can cut your toes off just as easily if you are not careful. I had never seen one and so, instead, I just used two pieces of line tied to the outside of the swim-step. To bring the dinghy aboard, I simply float the inflatable dinghy over the floating ropes, haul it up, and stow it vertically. My mistake was using polypropylene rope that had a breaking strength of about four hundred thousand pounds.

One afternoon, after refueling at Roche Harbor, I forgot to tie one of the lines securely as we were saying good-bye to a group of friends and backing away from the dock. The bitter end of one line was just the right length to get sucked into the starboard prop as I put the engine into reverse. I quickly found out something that, to the best of my knowledge, has never been written about. So, now you too can have total recall about handling cheapskate dinghy davits.

It is impossible to repair an inflatable dinghy that has been cut into two equal-size pieces athwartship by an ever-tightening piece of polypropylene rope. A rope that is wrapped around a stainless steel prop that is running in reverse at eleven hundred rpm's, in salt water that is 47 degrees Fahrenheit, with an ambient air temperature of 74 degrees.

Further, for your knowledge, the explosion of a nine-foot inflatable that has been hardened in the hot sun can be heard for approximately one and a half miles in still air.

And, yes, your ten-year fabric warranty is invalid when you stupidly cut your inflatable dinghy in half in this manner.

On the subject of engines for inflatable dinghies:

I traded a windsurfer, two pair of skis, and a rusty barbecue for a two-and-a-half horsepower, made-in-Japan, guaranteed-to-run-for-the-life-of-the-rope-that-you-yank-on-to-start-it outboard motor. It is an engine that will propel my inflatable at the speed of a Galapagos turtle (on land). The company that built the engine spent fifteen million dollars on research and development so it would be lightweight and compact.

As a result of the miniaturization of every component part, you get a gas tank the same size as that silver cup you bought for your firstborn with his name and birthday on it. This small tank guarantees that you can only get far enough away from your yacht so that it won't take over two hours to row back.

In my case, it took me three hours the first time we went sightseeing because of an unfavorable tide.

But it was okay because, when we finally got back, our boat was aground at low tide and I had other things to think about while we waited for the tide to come back in.

The remedy for this eight-ounce gas tank is to always take along a spare can of gas and a pair of oars. Be sure to take along an inflatable pump, because if you have to start rowing, your inflatable probably won't have enough air in it to support the oarlocks. They will sink down to water level with each stroke of the oars.

Oh yes! Also take along a water-pump, because I can guarantee you that when you take someone ashore, he will step out of the inflatable while it is up on a rock, and it is very hard to bail with the miniature funnel you brought along to refill the miniature gas tank.

If you plan on a hike while ashore, take along some spare food. Remember that the wind can come up and make it impossible to get back to your big boat. Where we cruise, a rifle and a cowbell should also be in your survival kit, in case you run across some black bears. Ring the bell while hiking so you don't surprise them. And you might as well bring along a tent in case you get lost and have to stay overnight. A thermal blanket is also a good idea. While you're at it, be on the lookout for a larger dinghy. Once you buy it, you will need a spacious, larger boat to carry the larger dinghy, a large set of davits to haul it aboard, and finally you will have to have a larger salary to support the new, larger boat that you have to buy.

The increase in your salary won't happen until you get a promotion, and are transferred to company headquarters in Kansas City, a land-locked city where you won't have a prayer of using all your new water toys. But, in that case, you won't have to worry about having total recall!

169

"The world revolves on equations."

THE WORLD REVOLVES
ON EQUATIONS

I was seventeen years old in 1942, when I signed up for college. I settled into a pattern of changing my major every semester until I finally dropped out when I was a senior. (I dropped out to spend the rest of my life in search of the elusive free ski lift ticket.) In 1943, I enlisted in the Navy V-12 Officer Training Program. In order to become an officer, I decided I needed all of the mathematics I could cram into my brain. In six semesters, I managed to enroll in and pass a variety of courses that included analytical geometry, differential calculus, integral calculus, astrophysics, and astronomy. For variety, I took classes in surveying, physics, life art, English, geology, and aerodynamics.

It didn't really matter what subjects I decided to take because I realized that World War II was already methodically killing most of the world's future leaders. The bravest and smartest men of all nations were the most patriotic, the first to enlist, and the first to begin shooting and getting shot at in front lines all over the world.

Most of the knowledge I gained is now obsolete and long ago has been buried in the folds of my brain. I would have to take a refresher course today, just to work a simple analytical geometry problem. But one simple equation I have never forgotten is an algebraic one, $E = MV^2$.

In my astrophysics course, I was taught the equation to calculate the pounds of thrust versus the weight of the rocket to generate the escape velocity necessary for a vehicle to leave earth's gravitational pull. Once we memorized the equation and passed the test, our professor told us to forget all about it because, in our lifetime, no one would be able to solve all the problems necessary to build a rocket big enough and light enough to escape the pull of earth's gravity.

How wrong he was.

I've long ago forgotten the escape velocity equation in my search for that always-elusive free lift ticket. However, I did learn one of life's basic, unalterable facts: *the world revolves on numbers and mathematical equations, and those equations never change.*

The following are a few math word problems and your assignment is to convert them to equations and come up with a finite answer:

The last summer Olympics in Atlanta had a budget of one-point seven billion dollars. (That's billion, not million.) The latest reports indicate that the organizers managed to break even on hosting the games. How did they reach the magic number of what they should charge for admission so they could break even? How did they figure out how much to charge for a hot dog and a Coca-Cola or a T-shirt?

How did they figure out that anyone who won a gold medal in an Olympic *amateur* track event could continue to be an *amateur* and be paid $50,000 just to show up at a future track meet and run or jump in their special event?

The United States Olympic Ski Team has an annual budget of $14,000,000. Or they did until they came up with a $1,800,000 shortfall. As a result, a lot of programs will be cut off, so some of the younger racers might have to pay their own way to their races.

Here's another mathematical equation for you to figure out: It has been reported that Picabo Street earns a million to a million-and-a-half-dollars a year as an Olympic *amateur* skier. What percentage of the ski team's $12,200,000 budget did your $25 donation go toward paying her room and board and what percentage goes to the administrative overhead of the team? What percentage of Picabo Street's million-and-a-half-dollars a year in endorsements is made available to train up-and-coming-junior racers?

More equations: If someone pays $50,000 for a reserved parking place at Gold Peak, how good a buy was a two-bedroom condominium across the street in 1967 for $45,000, and how much has it appreciated in contrast to the same amount invested in stocks and bonds with inflation factored in?

Here's a summer math problem:

If a man owns a thirty-five-foot fishing boat, how many salmon does he have to catch to buy the diesel fuel at $2.15 a gallon in Canadian currency, and be able to make his mortgage payment on the boat, and still have enough fuel left to get him the 83 miles back to the dock to sell his catch? (Canadian currency is valued at sixty-nine cents to the American dollar.)

Here's a simple math problem that many people will have to deal with this winter: If a couple rides round trip from Denver International Airport to Vail in a van, the cost is almost $200. The same two people can rent a car for that amount or less and have a car while they are spinning around the roundabout for the week. And, how much does it cost in addition to the $200,000 a year interest to retire the bonds so Steve and Susie Skier won't have to wait at a boulevard stop and can have their own car to help fill up the parking structure at $8 per day?

On-mountain mathematical equations can be more difficult to solve. Here's one: It costs x dollars to transport a snow cat load of food to the restaurant at the top of the mountain after trucking it from a city hundreds of miles away. What factor of the overall weight of the snow cat load of supplies does management apply to the cost of the bottle of Yuppie water, the chocolate chip cookie, and the hamburger that you buy?

If Steve, who is six-foot-five and weighs two hundred and forty-three pounds, spends $465 for his shaped skis, $375 for bindings, $415 for a new pair of boots, and $50 for a one-day lift ticket, how much does the resort have to pay to operate a $225,000 snow-grooming machine so Steve won't have to ski in bumps?

Basic math: How long does it take to find a parking place and get to the lift and stand in how-long a line at what time of the morning so you can meet your friends at Chairlift Nine at ten O'clock. (At lunch you find out you were supposed to meet them at Chairlift Ten at nine O'clock.)

Every one of these problems can be reduced to a mathematical equation that is very simple and always provides the same answer.

Income has to exceed outgo, or it is no go!

BLUE WATER FLIGHT

I'm retired so I don't have to fly as much as I used to, but I still knock off enough miles to get the occasional free upgrade. If there is such a thing anymore! In order to qualify for an upgrade, you have to call an 800 number two years in advance of your flight. Make sure you have a speakerphone because you will be put on hold for at least 4 hours for whatever reason they use that week. "All of our sales personnel are busy at this time. We cherish your business so please be patient. Due to the tremendous increase in our business at this time of the year, we have to put you on hold."

I had requested my travel agent to sell me my usual seat by an exit so I could have room to stretch my legs. No rooms for my arms, however, because the seats are so narrow. Years ago I learned how to turn the pages of a magazine or eat an airline meal while my elbows are touching in front of me.

On the other side of the exit was a washroom. In front of it were two people slowly mopping up water that was rapidly seeping out of the washroom.

In very poor English, one of the people who were trying to mop up the water kept saying, "Eet is coming out faster than I can mop eet up."

After five minutes of this, her partner said, "Let's get a vacuum and suck it up. Surely it can't leak out faster than that."

Five minutes of vacuuming, and it was still pouring out when the co-pilot came back and said very wisely, "Let's get a repairman and fix it before we take off."

The plane was already ten minutes late and we had lost our slot in the back-away-from-the-gate-get-lined-up-for-the-taxi-to-the-runway-to-wait-our-turn-to-take-off line.

In due time, the mechanic showed to up try to repair the leaking toilet. A leaking toilet was an assumption on my part because, whenever a stewardess walked down the aisle, the water that squished up around her shoes was blue.

The mechanic stared at the wet floor, said a few "Hmmmmmms," and then said, "This is a cinch to fix." Turning to the head flight attendant he said, "Anyone got a pencil, some paper, and a little scotch tape? I'll have this fixed in a moment." When the pencil, paper, and scotch tape arrived, he wrote, 'OUT OF ORDER,' and scotch-taped the note to the toilet door.

This prompted me to ask the flight attendant, "What happens when the plane takes off? Won't all of that blue water drip down through the floor where some rivets just might be loose and get my luggage all wet?"

"Our floors don't leak," the stewardess informed me. "Besides, this plane has to make connections in our Denver hub." My response was to gather up my gear and try to get off the plane. It turns out that is a federal offense to try to get off a commercial airplane while it is in motion. Regardless of its altitude!

My heart was in my mouth the entire trip to Denver, but even more so when we started down the runway and began to climb for altitude.

I had two pillows that I put down in the aisle to divert the flow of the blue water that came gushing out of the bathroom as the plane tilted up. There was enough blue water flowing down the aisle to reach clear to the back of the plane.

Just as the stewardess asked my name so she could report me for damaging the two pillows with the blue water, Captain Courageous showed up. I considered a flooded cabin an emergency, but apparently he didn't. He was very upset because the center of gravity of the airplane had shifted on take-off when 73 gallons of blue toilet flush flowed about 100 feet farther back. Let's see, 73 gallons times eight pounds to the gallon times 83 feet, is over 4,000 foot pounds of weight making the tail of the plane heavier than it should have been.

To compensate for this, the engineer and the captain had to crank a couple of unforeseen weights and balances into their on-board computer to make the plane level off without holding it there with their manual controls.

Once the captain knew what was wrong, he radioed Denver and all of the other airports in route that he didn't really have an emergency after all. All he had was a leaky toilet and some wet luggage.

When I deplaned in Denver, I had to stop in the men's room where I felt a little silly standing at the wash basin in my stocking feet washing the blue liquid off my brand new pair of white Nike's.

A friend of mine has the right idea. He says, "If I don't fly first class, my children will."

I'm gonna start doing that so I don't arrive with blue shoes.

You have to bring the small boat you were towing along-side the big boat. Then, when all of the fenders you own are put in between the two boats, you motor slowly into the marina and tie up to the dock.

ISLAND LIVING LOGISTICS

Living on a small island, as my wife and I do, requires the logistical skills of an army supply sergeant getting ready for the invasion of Normandy.

Last week I was going to Alaska to do some salmon fishing, but before my wife would let me go I (she) had a list of priorities: our small boat was not working smoothly; get the small boat fixed.

Our small fishing boat had engine problems. I never knew when it was going to start or just sit there and gloat over of my lack of mechanical skills.

Three days after I called our local handyman, he stopped by and, two hours, later diagnosed the problem as a coil that wasn't working.

Our bigger boat that we cruise to Alaska in needed some spring tune-ups and the water-maker motor needed replacing. It lived somewhere in the bowels of the mysterious engine room, an area I try not to visit if I can get away with it.

With all these boat problems, I also needed my car on the mainland so I could drive from Anacortes to Seattle so I could find an inexpensive motel to sleep in so I could fly to Alaska the next morning.

After a lot of discussion, my wife and I finally made the decision that I would drive the big boat and tow the little one the 25 miles to the boat yard. That way, the big boat could get fixed while I was trying to catch some Alaskan salmon and she would still have the little boat for transportation.

I managed to talk her into getting on the 10:30 ferry with the car that I would drive to Seattle.

Then, when they had replaced the coil on the small boat, she would drive that back to our island.

So far, so good!

When you are towing a boat to a dock, you have to stop out in the bay and bring the smaller boat alongside and tie it beside the bigger boat so you can maneuver both boats at the same time when and if you get near the dock. Similar to carrying your dog instead of hoping he will follow you on a 20-foot leash.

To do this, I had to put all the fenders I owned over the side, lead the tow line to the front of the big boat, and then tie the stern of the little boat firmly to the side of the big boat so it would go in whatever direction the big boat went.

The repair-yard foreman estimated that it would take about ten hours in the fiberglass shop to fix the small (relatively) dings and scratches that I had incurred. When they see me coming, they always have two fiberglass engineers available at the same time at their usual rate of $50 each per hour.

It's nice to be needed for the economy.

When both boats were finally tied up to the dock, the mechanic who charges the same rate per hour as my dentist and doctor came aboard and asked what the problem was.

I told the mechanic that, according to our local handyman, Joe, the engine was putting electricity into the coil but none of it was coming out.

My somewhat vague analysis of his diagnosis was that the recent three days in a row without rain had allowed whatever water had dripped into the coil to dry out and now the engine would only work on sunny days.

This is not a good option in this part of the

world, unless you don't mind having a boat that runs about fifteen percent of the time. Reluctantly, the mechanic said he would replace the coil.

While he went back up to the boat yard to get his 700-pound tool chest, I had an appointment with another mechanic to go over the things that needed fixing on our big boat. I had plenty of time to do this because I was waiting for my wife to arrive on the 12:30 ferry that would be its usual hour late.

When Laurie finally arrived, I took her to lunch in the best deli in town. While waiting in line, I discovered that it was almost the end of the spring semester and had been designated by the deli as "National-train-a-high-school-senior-to-make-sandwiches-day."

There were three people in line in front of us and so it only took 55 minutes to get a pair of cucumber, sprouts, peanut butter, sesame seed, and cream cheese sandwiches with pickles and chips on the side. Since a high school senior who had flunked beginning math many times was making it, he was having trouble figuring out how to make a two decker sandwich out of seven-grain bread.

The mechanic had the coil replaced on our small boat by the time we finished lunch.

I waved good-bye to Laurie as she headed out of the marina. I then I got ready to enter the real world of crowded freeways, smoggy sunsets, and also the relaxation of getting into an airport motel and watching one of the thousand or so playoff basketball games.

It had been over eighty degrees in Seattle that day and, after taking a shower, I eased back into the king-sized bed and got out the remote TV clicker, only to discover that the motel didn't have cable TV. My next discovery was that the air conditioner in my room didn't work. So I opened the window but, every time I nodded off to sleep, the roar of yet another jet taking off woke me up. Long after the Tonight Show had signed off, the only thing left on late-night television was a rerun of a feature-length ski movie I had produced in 1974. Since I had personally narrated it in over 100 different cities that year, it immediately put me to sleep.

The logistics of island living had certainly worn me out.

"Summer can mean different sounds to different people."

THE SOUNDS OF SUMMER

The violent sounds of an occasional dynamite blast can be heard in the distance. It sounds different than the dynamite charges that are set to trigger avalanches. Does it sound different because the sound is ricocheting off hard rock and standing timber instead of powder snow? Does it matter? Just get those ski lifts built in time for the first snowfall that is less than a hundred days away now.

For most skiers this time of the year, the sounds of skiing have been replaced by the sounds of iron against a golf club or gut against a fuzz covered tennis ball, or maybe the hum of a pair of knobby tires and the squeak of the brakes on your mountain bike as your speed exceeds your courage.

For Laurie and me, it is the sound of diesel engines throbbing in a fiberglass hull below us as we cruise through British Columbia on the inland-passage to Alaska.

I have been asked many times, "Doesn't just sitting there on the flying bridge and steering a big boat all day get boring?"

It depends on what comes by in the way of flotsam and jetsam, such as the time Laurie asked,

"Isn't that a boat on the rocks?"

"Sure is."

We put our small boat over the side to see if we could do anything for the stranded boaters until the tide came back in. Now the sounds change from the throb of the diesels to the high-pitched whine of the outboard motor and then the whimpering of the skipper of the boat that ran aground.

"Was your automatic pilot on?" I asked.

I call them "Automatic rock seekers." I won't have one on my boat. The skipper had finished folding a chart and went below for just a second to get an after-lunch beer, when the bow of his boat rose right up and there he was until the tide went the rest of the way out and back in again.

I appraised the damage to his boat as minimal, and said that he was very lucky that he went aground when the tide only had five or six feet to drop. There was no damage to the bottom of his boat and when the eleven feet of high tide came back in, he could float free and get on to his destination.

When his unidentified lady friend heard that I had notified the Canadian Coast Guard, she went ballistic, screaming,

"Call them back and cancel that report. I can't afford to be in the newspapers."

About that same time, a Canadian Fisheries boat cruised by and took over, so we headed on our quiet way north.

"Is that a branch floating, or a deer swimming?"

Looking through my binoculars, I saw two six-point bucks swimming from one island to another across about two miles of open water. After taking several photos of them, Laurie and I talked for a long time about what motivates a deer to swim from one island to another island that looks exactly like the island it just left. Maybe it has something to do with the doe population? Did you know that deer swim very gracefully? With unhurried strokes of their cloven hoofs, they look as though they are galloping in slow motion.

No sound whatsoever.

Being tied up to the Prince Rupert Rowing and Yacht Club for the night provides totally different sounds. Over 600 salmon fishing boats have to spend forty-eight hours in port so that some of the salmon can get through to go on up the rivers and spawn. Six hundred boats equal about two thousand fishermen. Give or take nineteen or twenty-three. Some caught a lot of fish, some didn't. Some got drunk, most didn't. The impossible sounds of the Vietnamese-speaking fishermen dominate the silence of most of us who tend to observe rather than comment. These hard working fishermen don't play tennis, golf, or go mountain-bike riding during their days off. You can just hear the sounds of tools as they repair any of the gear that needs to be ready for the next opening of fishing forty-eight hours from now.

At 2:30 am, we were jolted awake by a lot of hollering and sirens wailing. It was the harbor police with spotlights shining, chasing a fishing boat that was spinning circles in the harbor and, with each round trip, getting closer and closer to the boats moored at the dock. With our engines still cold, we got away from the dock just before the fishing boat bounced off almost the same spot we had just been occupying. Aboard the fishing boat was a very drunken fisherman having a very violent fight with a Royal Canadian Mounted Policeman.

No one was steering the boat!

On the fourth round trip, the Mountie finally knocked out fisherman. He did it with the club the fisherman uses to kill his fish when he brings them aboard.

The Mounties always get their man!

Last night, we anchored in a thirteen-mile-long, very quiet fjord called Khutzeymateen. Near the

185

head of the fjord, we watched as seven grizzly bears silently munched on salt-water grass in the evening light.

As we rounded the final corner, there was only one boat at anchor.

And what a boat it was.

Built by Britisher, Sir T.O.M. Sopwith, who also built the best warplanes flying for the Allies during World War One. He had his boat built as a challenger for The America's Cup in 1934. Restored in 1989, for approximately ten million dollars by Elizabeth E. Meyer, it is 130 feet long with a mast 165 feet high. I can easily see why it has been called, "The most magnificent sailboat afloat in the world today." As we cruised by, admiring it, I was imagining, "I am steering it with 9,000 square feet of canvas aloft and charging for the starting line of an America's cup race." At the same time, we were also looking for a safe spot to anchor when our boat ground to an abrupt stop.

The ugly sound of an expensive pair of propellers gouging their way through mud and sand, instead of good, clean, salt water is a sound I hope I never have to hear again as long as I am aboard a boat of any kind.

At low tide this morning, I took the dinghy over to the sand bar and silently walked to where our propeller marks were still carved in the mud. They were almost two hundred feet from the water's edge, and eight feet above where the water now was.

I stood there with my camera in my hand but decided not to take a picture of this, just one more of my many lurches from one near disaster to the next. Instead, I just wept openly, when the full impact of what a simple mistake could have led to.

Had we been unable to back our boat off the

sand and mud, it would have been a two or three thousand dollar towing job to get us off, assuming nothing was bent or broken in the shafts, struts, or props.

Weeping after grounding any boat is a normal reaction. It sounds, and is, a lot worse than crossing your tips in deep powder snow, or missing a golf ball or a tennis ball, or the squeak of your brakes over the whistle of the wind through your brain bucket as you depart your mountain bike over the handlebars of your mountain bike.

Any of these sounds can be boring - unless you are listening to them at the time they are being created by you.

I suppose, by now, that I should be accustomed to the sounds I make as I lurch from one near disaster to the next. But, I'm not! I always think that the last one will be the LAST one, so I'm always surprised by the NEXT one. Oh well, at least I haven't lost my hearing – yet!

WARREN MILLER '98

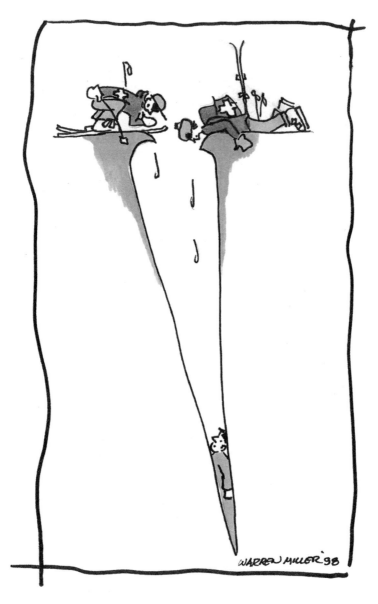

"I've been down here for three days. Where've you guys been?"

CREVASSE

The gondola is crowded this morning as it climbs rapidly in the clear blue French sky. On board are seventy-five other snowboarders and skiers. I had tried to be on the first gondola on the upper section this morning, but it was not to be. With a lot of pushing and shoving, I have managed to get onto the third gondola load because there have been a lot of people who think they should automatically go ahead of us. The twenty-two inches of powder snow has gotten everyone in town up early. Waiting in line has taken longer than normal because of the early birds with inside connections. Private instructors with their pupils and spousal equivalents of ski patrolmen are already crowding in line ahead of me for their second run in the untracked powder.

The upper gondola of Super Chamonix has a cable speed of almost twenty miles an hour so, once onboard, the ride takes less than ten minutes for the five thousand vertical foot climb. As it sways gently from its glide over the main tower, we can see a group of four skiers traversing over the top of one of the best slopes on this vast, undulating, steep glacier. Not another ski track is yet visible on the West Side of the gondola except their traverse marks.

Under the foot and a half of light powder snow that fell last night is a glacier of rock-hard ice that is over five hundred feet deep in places. It is criss-crossed by deep crevasses. The giant sea of ice moving slowly down the hill causes these crevasses. The mile-long sea of ice doesn't bend, but instead breaks as the mountain it covers changes the course of the ice as it moves. The crevasses are sometimes as wide as a hundred feet or so, or as narrow as an inch or two and sometimes seemingly limitless in their depth.

When it snows hard, the blowing snow will form a cornice on one side of the crevasse and, when the wind changes direction, it will form another cornice on the other side of the crevasse. The two cornices will get larger and larger until they sometimes touch and form a bridge of snow. There is nothing under it except a bottomless killer-void of freezing cold air called a crevasse. Where the two cornices meet is sometimes only an inch or two thick, so when a skier goes across one, the fragile bridge of snow can give way and skiers can fall to their death.

I was explaining all of this to my wife as I watched the four skiers traversing the glacier. One of the ladies in the group who was wearing a canary-yellow parka was traversing a little higher than the other three when she suddenly disappeared, her long traverse tracks ending in a black hole the size of a pair of skis and her body.

Fortunately, the conductor on the Gondola witnessed the accident and quickly dialed the ski patrol. Before we arrived at the top station, the ski patrol was on its way down to attempt a rescue.

For me, this was a good opportunity to get some rare rescue shots for a magazine article I was writing at the time. I skied down as fast as I could in the deep powder snow; by the time I got to the accident, half of the ski patrol was engaged in crowd control. There was at least half a dozen other ski patrolmen who had already rigged their rescue ropes and lowered one of the patrolmen down into the crevasse. The word he sent up from deep in the crevasse was encouraging. It was a lady who had fallen in. She was down about forty-five feet, perched precariously on a narrow ledge of ice that fortunately was covered with about five feet of powder snow. She was stunned, but still alive.

For the next ten minutes there was much hollering back and forth from the patrolman who was in charge to the one down in the crevasse who was actually doing all of the rescue work.

A few minutes later, the head patrolman said something in untranslatable French and the five remaining patrolmen began sidestepping down the hill. They all had a good grip on the rope that led down to the lady in the crevasse.

When the victim finally was dragged over the lip of the crevasse, we were all shocked to discover that it wasn't the lady in the yellow parka that we had expected to see.

Instead, on the end of the rope was a man.

He had fallen into the crevasse two days earlier and was near death from hypothermia. Fortunately, he had been wearing a thick down parka over his powder snowsuit and long underwear under it. He also had two candy bars with him and the combination had saved his life. However, he had wasted away to virtual skin and bones while down there. He looked like he had lost twenty pounds during his two-day ordeal in the darkness of the sub-zero crevasse.

When this hypothermia-caused-weight-loss information was passed back down to the ski patrolman who was still in the crevasse, a heated argument was heard between the patrolman and the lady who was still down there.

She had figured out that the guy they had hauled up first had lost twenty pounds while he was down there, so she hollered back up, "Come back and get me in a couple of days!"

191

"That raccoon caught the rock I had thrown, threw it
right back at me, and hit me right between the eyes."

THE INVASION OF
THE RACCOONS

This is how Webster's dictionary defines raccoon: 'A small flesh-eating mammal of North America that is chiefly gray in color, has a bushy, ringed-tail and lives chiefly in trees.'

There have been hundreds of magazine articles and dozens of books written about this very unusual-looking animal.

People talk in frustration about the raccoon's ability to unscrew the lid of a mason jar and get at the jam, jelly, or peanut butter that is inside, or untie the rope or wire that has been put around the garbage can lids.

People have written in Reader's Digest about losing their pet dog and cats to this harmless-looking animal with the black, masked eyes. Daniel Boone made the raccoon famous with one of their tails hanging down from his cap. In his case, that raccoon's demise probably served a good purpose by keeping the flies off the back of his neck.

While in Denver recently, I received a frantic phone call from my wife that one of the local raccoons had killed our pet goose, a wonderful bird that she was fattening for our next Thanksgiving dinner.

Sure enough, the raccoons had removed a two pound rock from on top of a 2x6 piece of lumber that was leaning against the plywood door of the cage as an added protection from raccoons. Then they had lifted up the door of the cage and had gotten inside and had an early Thanksgiving dinner. We were now believers of the Reader's Digest article we had read a couple of years ago about how intelligent raccoons are.

When I got home two days later, sure enough, the goose was dead and the raccoons had arrived on our property like your second cousin's family from Arkansas. Four or five of them would cruise in every evening looking for food scraps, and anything else that was edible. Yes, they can turn over garbage cans, they can get the lid off one even if you tie it with a rope, and they can keep our dog barking whenever they are within 100 feet of the house.

Four or five days later, at about 11:00 p.m., I was just getting out of the shower when my wife, Laurie, started hollering,

"Come out here and help me get the raccoons out of the bird feeder!"

About the only thing my wife can't do is to throw a rock with any accuracy. Rocky the Raccoon just watched her throwing rocks and finally climbed slowly and deliberately down the wire deer fence alongside the bird feeder.

It was almost dark by now, and I had to protect my family from this animal that was putting terror in the hearts of our dog, cat, and garbage can. So, with a towel wrapped around my still-dripping, soap-covered body, I rose to the occasion and proved that I too, couldn't break a window with a rock if I was inside the house and trying to throw it outside.

That raccoon just wandered over to a nearby tree and slowly climbed about twenty feet up. There, it sat on a limb and looked down at me with that "I dare you to try to come up and get me" look that all raccoons give semi-naked, wet, soap-covered, bath-toweled men as midnight approaches.

He just sat there on that limb while my wife

hollered at me to do something.

Having studied trajectories of ballistics in a Navy Gunnery course in 1943, I knew that if I lobbed a one-pound rock up at that raccoon at an 81-degree angle from the horizontal, I could, in all probability, hit him in the fanny. If I connected, he might decide to go down the street to someone else's bird feeder and goose cage.

I told my wife to stand back just in case I hit him hard enough to knock him out of the tree. Then, I gave that one-pound rock my best underhand softball pitch straight up in the air at that smiling raccoon.

Somehow, I lost sight of the rock in the dark branches of the tree.

But, what happened a moment later makes me believe all of the raccoon stories I have ever heard. One of two things had to have happened.

1. That raccoon caught the rock and threw it back at me, or

2. I was a little off on my selection of trajectory angle and I lobbed the rock straight up into the air and it came straight back down.

That one-pound rock came hurtling back down out of the darkness and hit me right between the eyes. It hit me hard enough to knock me right down onto my knees on the gravel driveway. (Fortunately, my towel was long enough to cover my knees, so I didn't scuff them up when I folded.)

The raccoon just sat up on that limb hissing at me.

Or, was he giving me the raspberries?

My wife was trying to attend to my profusely bleeding wound, but she almost passed out from laughing so hard.

The next night, I had to explain my black eye and the lump the size of a golf ball on my forehead to an audience in Boulder, Colorado, when I was introducing the preview of our new ski movie.

If that raccoon had been in the audience, he probably would have hissed at my movie, too!

Golf is a game that is almost as dumb as skiing, but is played by older people.

GOLF, ANYONE?

It's that time of the year when you wonder where the white went when the snow melted. If you are old enough, you are probably shining up the new set of golf clubs you bought last winter.

With dozens of fine golf courses spread throughout New England, you can play golf at a lot of them and look up at the nearby ski runs where you spent most of your money last winter.

Now you can spend what is left of it by visiting a different golf course every weekend all summer.

Golf is a game that is as dumb as skiing, but is played by older people.

There are a lot of words in the English language, that, spelled backward, still spell a recognizable word but mean something completely different.

For example: stop is pots spelled backwards. Tums becomes smut, words like that. Golf to me means the same thing either way because 'flog' is what I do to a golf ball.

There is a low-budget golf course here on my island that is complete with greens that vary between bowling-alley smoothness and wind-driven ocean waves. The fairways vary between being as hard as an asphalt highway and maybe one made of concrete. They depend on rain for their green color and sun for their growth. We have had only two days of rain in the last three months, so the fairways are about the color of a piece of whole-wheat bread with a dab of peanut butter here and there.

I do not pretend to be a golfer. I don't even

197

know how to keep score. The last time I played in 1968, we kept track of our good shots and the guy with the most good shots was the winner. My partner won because he had five good shots.

The other day, a friend of mine was holding a golf tournament for 22 of his weekend houseguests and invited me to help fill out a foursome. I immediately dug around in my garage and found my nearly new, hardly-ever used, Arnold Palmer 1968 set of matching clubs. They were buried under half a dozen crab traps that didn't work too well, behind the band saw, alongside the drill press, and under the outboard motor that seized when I forgot to add oil to the gasoline four years ago.

I arrived in the golf course parking lot, properly dressed in matching short pants and the only golf shirt I own. It just happened to say Johnson Evinrude on the shirt pocket. I have had it ever since they still put pockets on golf shirts. After meeting 22 people whose names I didn't bother remembering because I will never see them again, I was put together in a foursome that was starting last. I thought getting to start last was in deference to our ages. The four of us totaled 274 years, six years of which had something to do with golf.

As I dragged my golf bag out of the car, I vaguely remembered having put a pair of golf shoes away after the last time I played golf, in the fall of 1968. A friend of Jean Claude Killy's agent had given the clubs to me because he was also Arnold Palmer's agent. (I thought I would drop some names before I tell you about the fifth round of golf in my life.)

The beautiful island golf course charges a green fee of $15 and to rent a cart is $3 more. Electric ones are $15 but no one rented them because they run on gasoline and have a rope to yank on to start them each time.

Four years ago they raised the green fee from $10 to $15 and half the people on the island quit playing because it got too expensive.

Back to the tournament.

I dug around in my golf bag with its nineteen zippers and found my long-forgotten golf shoes. When I tried to put them on, I remembered that the last time I had worn them, in 1968, we had to quit because it was raining too hard and I must have just stuffed the shoes in the bag along with my wet grass-covered socks. The shoes were now two-thirds full of what looked like a science experiment in growing some rare, mutant, green-and-gold-colored moss. The moss was easily dug out with my sand wedge and then the shoes fit quite comfortably. There was no room for my socks, however.

While foursome after foursome teed off, I began to feel like the last person who mistakenly got invited to a dinner party, and the only adult eating a sit-down dinner on a card table in the hall with the hostess's three step-children.

I thought the other three in our foursome were good players. It turned out that they were not very good players, but black-diamond caliber compared to my snowplow turns.

Six years ago, I had purchased a couple of dozen recycled golf balls at a discount sporting goods store when I had decided that I wanted to learn how to juggle. Since we were only playing nine holes, I figured that eighteen out of the twenty-four balls would be enough for me to bring along to some-how slash my way around the course.

By the seventh hole, I had run out of golf balls and the other guys in my foursomes were charging me $5 per ball and standing way back watching me hit them in every direction. They also convinced me that the red stripes around the balls made them more valuable.

I think they called the tournament Best Ball or Scrambled Eggs or Old Maid, or some such thing. At any rate, I never did hit any of my rapidly dwindling supply of balls anywhere except into the trees or into the lake or onto the highway alongside the course. I always got to hit last. By the second hole, the rest of my foursome were standing well back from the tee just in case I magically hit one 90 degrees from where it was supposed to go.

I came close to doing just that a couple of times.

When we finally staggered into the clubhouse after our nine holes, the host and his 22 houseguests were gone, and the course Pro and his current girl-friend were snuggled up on a sagging couch, watching the TV set that was situated over the sign pointing to the men's room.

He turned to us and said, "They left a trophy for you and a map of how to get to their house."

The trophy said, "Highest Gross."

Whatever that means!

WASH AND WEAR, WHEREVER

When I led ski tours to Europe during the early 1950's, it was my sole responsibility to provide everything my customers might want during their trip. If it was not as advertised, or I could not provide it, it was always my fault. For example, I was supposed to provide the following things to my customers, but not necessarily in this order:

1. An airplane that took off and landed at the right rate of speed.

2. Impeccable food and service in flight.

3. No frustrating hassles at check-in because of overweight luggage exemptions.

4. Trains that left and arrived on time.

5. Super hotel rooms within walking distance of the ski lifts, and no lift lines.

6. Beautiful, foxy ladies for the guys and handsome, single ski instructors for the ladies.

7. Baggage handlers and ski waxers.

8. Exactly the right kind of snow and clear, cold, blue skies every day and snowstorms every night.

9. I had to know where all the just-right, quaint restaurants were and have reservations for same every night.

10. How to get bargains on anything from ski pants and parkas to gold watches, including, but not limited to, Swiss wood carvings, Austrian Lederhosen, Chocolate factories, and French Wine.

11.Supply people who spoke impeccable English for my charges.

While the trip was going on, I was also trying to gather footage for my next feature-length ski film and somehow find an hour or two a night to sleep. Oh yes, one evening at each resort we visited I would show my then current, feature-length film. Those were the days when I played a tape recorder for musical backup and narrated the film presentation live. Europe, however, was using 220 volts and fifty-cycle electricity, instead of 110-volt, sixty-cycle. As a result, my tape recorder played about seventeen percent slower than it should. When I was narrating the film, I had to fast-forward to the appropriate music and hope it cut in where it should match the film when I turned it back on.

Tickets to see the film were twenty-four Austrian shillings or four Swiss francs. In 1954, that was about the equivalent of a dollar. The same hotel I would show the film in would charge $3 to wash a shirt, $6 to clean and press a suit and $4 a night to rent a room, including three meals and a bath down the hall.

Enter Wash and Wear.

It didn't take me very long to learn in those days that I could haul around clean clothes for every day of the trip, or I could take two pair of everything.

I only took a complete week's supply of clean clothes to Europe once. I found out that after the first week everything I brought along was dirty, the laundry took four days and cost a fortune, and I had to leave for the next resort before it got washed, ironed, and returned to me anyway.

Being a creative cheapskate has always been one of my strong points. Every dollar I was able to save on necessities, I was able to set aside to purchase more sixteen-millimeter film for my already insatiably thirsty motion-picture camera.

The second year I traveled to Europe, I approached things differently. After a day of skiing, it was very easy to get into the shower in my T-shirt and long underwear or my jockey shorts, and wash each one of them before completely undressing and washing the rest of me. After they were washed and rinsed, I would simply ring 'em out, hang 'em up, and proceed with my shower. The same wash and wear applied to my dress shirts. I had two white, nylon dress shirts that I could wash, hang up on a clothes hanger, button the top button, straighten out the collar and they would be as clean and neat looking as if they had just come back from the laundry. A laundry that in many of the villages we stayed in was someone's wife who walked three miles from her farmhouse to get your laundry, washed it on a scrub board, hung it up outside to dry, and then two days later walked three miles back to your hotel to return it. Unless any of their farm animals had a problem. Then, forget ever seeing your laundry again.

As a result of those early days of wash and wear, I have come up with some tips for your ski trip:

Set fifteen minutes aside each night to do your laundry or else you will wind up hauling a suitcase or two of dirty clothes all around the country.

Don't be afraid to take only two pair of ski pants and two parkas. That way, you have four different combinations of clothes to present to the skiing world. A sweater or two, and you are in business.

Another thing I learned a long time ago is that no one pays any attention to you on a ski hill that is full of world-class skiers. The level of ski competence today is so high that unless you have won a six-pack of world-cup freestyle events, no one notices you.

Evening dress is another thing. Being in the necktie business today has to be about as profitable as being in the brassiere business would have been in the 1960's. No one wears a tie to anything anymore. I think they call it "mountain casual." That means wear anything you have left in your duffel bag that is clean. Levi's, sweater, cowboy shirt, your high school letterman's sweater - it doesn't matter. Unless you go to a tonier restaurant, then you can dress just like you are going to a Halloween party, only without a mask. There is no way you can plan on what to pack to eat out every night. If you are afraid, put a sport coat or a knit-dress in your duffel bag. To get it pressed, hang it on a clothes hanger in the bathroom and turn on the hot shower for ten minutes. This will steam up the bathroom to such an extent that your coat will hang out like it just came back from the dry cleaners.

Some people feel they have to have a different ski outfit for every day of the week. When I met my wife Laurie at the top of Mt. Baldy in Sun Valley, I was wearing a seven-year-old White Stag, green vest from which 98% of the feathers had long-ago crept out from under the duct-tape that was supposed to seal up the rips and tears in it.

For me, the feeling of making a turn down the side of a hill has always been where it's at, rather than the exterior covering of a body that has had all of its warranties expire. Personally, my warranty is "Wash and Wear, Wherever!"

THIRTEEN IS A
LUCKY NUMBER

We had spent a couple of days relaxing in Sullivan Bay after our first boat trip to Alaska. We had just completed our inaugural trip in our new boat and it was nice to have made it back around Cape Caution without a mishap or even bad weather in either direction.

I have spent a lot of time reading horror stories of this forty miles of the Inland Passage to Alaska because it is the only stretch of water that is not inland and not protected. It is wide open to any weather that might occur between where you are and where the warm summer waters of the Japanese currents collide with the ice-cold Bering Sea. There is some good weather here, but mostly bad. You can worry about fog, sudden storms, and big ground swells, as well as any one of the more than one million things that can go wrong with your boat during any ocean passage. (And they only go wrong when you are using them.)

Our boat was almost new and surprisingly free of defects, except those that occur because of our lack of experience in operating it properly. Like hitting logs or rocks.

We left Big Bay early in the morning and intended to put a lot of miles under our hull that day. Laurie was anxious to get back to our island home and see if her garden had survived her automatic watering system.

We were headed south late in the day, about ten miles southeast of Cape Mudge in the Strait of

Georgia, when we saw a salmon fishing boat dead in the water.

We altered course and came alongside and were very surprised to find that there were only two young boys on board. They had run out of fuel. They then told us that their father had gotten off in Campbell River to fly home because their mother had to have her appendix taken out.

We lay to alongside for awhile and then took them in tow and headed for Lund. I knew that they could get fuel there and, if their father trusted them with his fishing boat, I sure would trust one of them to steer their boat properly while it was tied onto a long rope behind my boat.

By my calculations, we would still get to Lund before total darkness but not before the fuel dock shut down for the night. We took the younger of the two aboard our boat. He told us that his older brother was thirteen and that the two of them had been fishing with their father in Alaska for the last four years. The first summer they were eight and nine years old, so they already had more power-boating experience than I did.

While we were motoring along in very calm weather, Laurie went below and made up a big dinner for everyone and, before I knew it, our young passenger was sound asleep in the main cabin.

When we tied up at Lund a little after 10pm, it was almost dark. Everything around the dock was secured, so we all fell into bed exhausted.

At breakfast, the real story about their father flying home from Campbell River began to unravel.

We learned that their father had died of a heart attack between Ketchikan and Alert Bay while trying to land a fifty-three pound salmon. The thirteen-year-old boy wasn't sure about the legality of burying someone at sea. What would happen if the Canadian government found out? Would they impound their boat? How could they prove he had just dropped dead? Why hadn't they radioed for help? How much would it cost to fly their mother to Alert Bay and she and their dad's body back to Seattle? A thousand unanswered questions rattled around in their teenage minds.

After a long conversation, the two of them decided that the best thing to do was to take him back to Seattle with them. He had died when they had about a thousand pounds of fish on board and plenty of ice.

Little as they were and as heavy as their father's body was, they somehow were able to drag him alongside the fish hold. Then one of them climbed down into the hold and moved their cargo of fish around until there was a space large enough for their dad's body. Once they were able to get him below and lying on the bed of fish and ice, they simply covered him with salmon and ice.

No, they had not called their mother because they didn't want her to worry. Yes, they had driven the boat all the way south from the Alaska border and thought that they had enough fuel to get all the way home. Yes, they had forgotten about the strong currents that they might have in Johnstone Strait and other places along the way.

They were safely tied up to the dock and no one knew about their father's death. Why bring the Canadian government into the problem? A day's journey south and the three of them would be almost in their homeport in the States.

We left well enough alone and wished them well. As we motored away from the dock, I tried to remember what I was capable of doing when I was thirteen years old.

My former partners said, "We've hired the best voice coach available in proper English to spend a week with you to work on your diction and, most important, your timing and delivery."

IF IT AIN'T BROKE, DON'T FIX IT

I have to turn back the clock six or seven years to when I had some partners in my film business. We had been partners for almost five years and they had brought a lot of management and growth to the company in such a short time. I was looking forward with eagerness to celebrating my fortieth year of walking out onto the stage and introducing my new feature-length ski film.

I had just finished two weeks of wonderful wind-blowing-just-right windsurfing right off the beach in front of our place in Maui. That is, if you consider trying to commit geriatric genocide by trying to windsurf round-trip from Maui to Molokai in marginal winds with a couple of other senior citizens and living to tell the tale.

Later that night, in a state of complete exhaustion and near-terminal sunburn, I caught the red eye from Kahalui, Maui, to Los Angeles. I got to ride in the back between two Sumo wrestlers who were on their way to a qualifying match in Fresno, California. I was headed for Hollywood to supervise the mixing of my recorded and edited narration, the music, and the images that would eventually become our new feature-length ski film. The recording, or dubbing as it is called, took a couple of extra days because of last-minute changes in the musical score of the new film and the insistence of change on the part of some of the new executives in what was no longer my film company. It was now "our" film company and "subtle changes" were taking place daily.

The day after we finished the dubbing was semi-uneventful. Then, it was off to lunch with the man who was the president of "our" film company. For the first time, he brought along his assistant to join us.

The lunch went well, but I could tell that there was some underlying current of unrest on their minds.

Our discussions ran the gamut from: should the company move out of its headquarters in Hermosa Beach to larger quarters in Beverly Hills, to what about just remodeling, to what should we film the following season for the next feature film, to what about the long-awaited trip to Antarctica to film?

Finally, I said,

"There's something on your minds and lets get it out on the table."

"Warren, we want you to set the last week of September aside because we have a surprise for you."

My mind raced ahead a bit as I tried to imagine what the great surprise was going to be. A trip to Europe as a bonus for a job well done? Maybe a new car? A trip to Disneyland? I could use a new roof on my building. What I needed most was a new chair for my desk. The chair was now seventeen years old and a little bent and tattered.

"You're really going to like this surprise we have for you because we know that you are always interested in growth and improving the product."

(Oh, oh. Sounds like a setup of some kind. I was born at night, but not last night)

"We have made a reservation for you in Carmel for that week. The Bed and Breakfast is off the beaten path and very, very quiet. We have gone to great expense to reserve the best voice coach in

California to spend that week with you so he can improve your voice, your timing, and your delivery while you are narrating your films."

Taken aback, my reply was,

"Huh?"

Then I stuttered a bit and mumbled,

"I'll have to think about it and see if I can fit it into my very busy schedule. I really think there's a windsurfing regatta that weekend that I have qualified for."

It sounded like a reasonable excuse to me to stall for thinking time.

In slightly less than two seconds, I had my mind made up.

If this was all that my partners and the president of my film company knew about why my ski films had been successful for forty consecutive years, I probably shouldn't renew my employment contract with them when it came up for negotiation in three months.

And I didn't.

I'm still writing and narrating the films the same way I have done them since the first time I walked out on the stage in October of 1950.

My philosophy is, "If it ain't broke, don't try to fix it.

Laurie named her goose, Thanksgiving Dinner.
Three months later, the raccoons made it their
Fourth-of-July-dinner.

MY WIFE'S GEESE

Whether or not you believe in reincarnation, I believe my wife's previous life was as the mistress of the barnyard somewhere in the dark ages. For a lady born and raised in the city, she has a passion for raising ducks, chickens, and any other farm animals the local feed store can unload upon her.

A few years ago when I came home from a trip, she had a baby goose living in our bathtub at night. She was afraid the raccoons would kill it if she left it outside. I don't mind the ceaseless noises of geese all night, but their smell is another thing!

She named her new goose Thanksgiving Dinner, but about three months later the raccoons made it their Fourth of July dinner. In the three months of its life, that goose probably cost me about $250, everything included. Special goose-feeding dispenser, special goose-watering tank, and a very special goose cage that our local handyman spent four-and-a-half days building at a cost of his wages plus about $145 for building supplies from the local lumber yard.

The next year when we got back from a winter of skiing, Laurie bought two geese, one for her and one for our next door neighbor. She had wisely figured that when we went on a trip, our neighbor could take care of her goose and she could take care of the neighbor's when she went away for the weekend. Our neighbor's husband raises racing pigeons; at least he did until the night she put both geese in his pigeon cage. One raccoon managed to somehow

213

get into his pigeon cage and kill both geese and several pigeons. The raccoon had an overweight friend, so he shoved the second goose over to the edge of the cage where the second raccoon had pried one of the chicken wire holes a little bigger. Then, he just stuck his hand and arm through the hole and devoured most of the second goose.

Last year was a little better. Some sort of virus had decimated the raccoon population on the island, so Laurie's Christmas Dinner goose spent the summer growing bigger by the month while following her all over our property. After almost a year of buying that goose the best food that our Visa card could afford, I finally named it the Greyhound Goose. That sucker could flap its wings and run faster than our dog. Then, all fall long, he didn't put on more than four or five ounces of sinewy muscle instead of plump Christmas Dinner meat. So Laurie decided he was too small and too pretty to eat.

Our handyman roasted him instead, while we were gone for the winter, and now we are into another farm animal cycle.

The other day when I stopped at the local hardware-lumber-yard-gas-station-nursery-and-feed-store, there was a message from my wife to, "Be sure to pick up the animals."

Two baby geese *and* thirteen baby chicks!

In one evening, when they were less than three weeks old, a raccoon or a wild mink ate eleven of the baby chickens and one of the geese.

Since then, our handyman has spent the last two weeks building a chicken coop that he claims, "Anyone on the FBI's ten most-wanted list couldn't break into, much less a raccoon." We'll see.

Laurie has ordered enough replacement chickens and geese, however, so that the cost of the first dozen eggs is now down to a little less than $645, if in fact they survive until they're six months old when they start laying eggs.

While she's waiting for our handyman to finish the new "Taj Mahal of chicken-coop condos," every night my wife puts all twenty, chirping, quacking animals into a large plastic bucket and transfers them into our bathtub (no water). The tub now has a special incubator heat lamp (another $19) that keeps them from shivering during the short hours of darkness. (Fortunately, we have a separate shower.)

Our handyman says he only has two more week's work to do on the chicken coop. This will include: the wiring for the special heat lamps, piped-in music so they will rest better at night, an infrared light to detect raccoons or any other predator coming near the coop in the dark, and a specially designed water dispenser (with water warmed up, of course). She has also ordered a special food dispenser from the Martha Stewart catalog. And, naturally, that chicken coop will have to be stained to match the antique look of the rest of her garden. This is a must, so it will look like it has been there as long as the abandoned foundation for the old house she has built her garden in and around.

At dinner with friends last night, she let it slip that she found a wonderful stained-glass window to use to make a transom over the door for ventilation and to help the chickens feel a little more special. That's what we need, chickens with culture.

Laurie tries to tell me that she is happier with her menagerie than if I was to buy her untold diamonds and pearls. However, if and when the first chicken survives to lay the first egg, for the same amount of money I could have bought a Faberge egg from the original collection of Czar Nicholas the First, of Russia.

"I spent 1962 to 1984, racing a variety of sailboats. Then I found out that there was another kind of boat that was pushed through the water with an engine."

THE WIND IN YOUR FACE

Elmo and his wife Ruby, who live on the other side of the island from us, bought their first sailboat last week. It's a small one, 21-feet long. The salesman told them, "While you're at it, you better buy a small outboard motor to get home with when the winds drops to zero or the tide is running against you."

Thus armed with a book on how to sail, a road map of the various islands, and their daughter Prosperity, they set out the other day on their very first sailing adventure. The wind was brisk as they sat nervously at the dock trying to figure out how to hoist the sail.

Later that evening, I got the full report of their first day with the wind in their sails and the spray in their face.

They had somehow managed to sail downwind, over to a bigger island for lunch in a brisk west wind and a following current. There, they managed to lower the sail and tie up into the marina.

By the time they finished lunch, the tide had changed and the wind had dropped to about 3mph, just enough wind so they could sail away from the dock and about halfway home. As the wind dropped to zero, Elmo lowered the 'just-in-case' outboard motor into the water. Finally moving smartly through the water at about 6mph, Ruby and Prosperity both had thoughts of, "Why didn't we buy a motor boat instead of a sailboat." But with Captain Elmo at the tiller and throttle, neither dared speak of such a radical idea. Within a mile, the engine died. Thirty-five minutes later, Prosperity discovered it had died from lack of gasoline. Unfortunately, most outboard motors take a proper mixture of gasoline and oil to continue to run. Frantic waving by the Elmo Crumb family stopped the first five powerboats that came by. Unfortunately, all of them were headed in the wrong direction, or had no pre-mixed gasoline with them.

Elmo finally remembered that Ruby had her cellular phone on board and so he called a friend on a nearby island to see if they would put a couple of gallons of pre-mix gasoline on board their run-about and come out and help them get home.

During the winter, Elmo lives in Miami, Florida, so his cellular phone started roaming and roaming and roaming, until after about $37 in charges, it finally located his friend who lives on the same island. His friend has call forwarding and wasn't home.

Fortunately, his friend also had the new technology where the incoming call will search for you wherever you are, until you answer one of your phones. This time his friend happened to be on a fact-finding mission in Helsinki, Finland, for his consulting company. A Finnish laborer picked up the phone because Elmo's friend was way up on a scaffold inspecting some asbestos in the ceiling. By this time, almost an hour of cellular phone time had been racked up searching all over the world for him. Through an interpreter, Elmo finally got Wolfgang's assistant, Clyde, to get him down off the scaffold and explained what his problem was. This took another ten minutes of cellular roaming and waiting time. It was then that Elmo finally figured out where Wolfgang was and realized that two gallons of pre-mixed gasoline in Helsinki wasn't going to do much good to power a sailboat in the San Juan Islands of Washington state.

Wolfgang suggested that Elmo call me, but he didn't have my phone number with him while he was up on the scaffold in Helsinki. Since I have an unlisted local number, he remembered that I had sold my film company to my son in Boulder, Colorado, and Elmo might get my local number from him. This meant another fifteen minutes of roaming and when Elmo finally got that Boulder number from information and dialed it, the recorded message that answered tried to sell him a copy of my latest ski video.

This is when the 6:30 ferry stopped because a crewman saw Elmo and Ruby waving, while Prosperity hung over the side doing what people do when they're seasick. Elmo was waving and listening on his cellular phone call to Boulder, Colorado, when the ferryboat crew put a rescue boat over the side. There was a lengthy consultation between the ferryboat rescue team and Elmo, while 160 carloads of people waited impatiently on the ferry to be even later to wherever they were eventually going than they usually are.

There was some pre-mix outboard motor fuel on board the ferryboat, and the law of the seas says that you have to help someone in trouble. The rescue boat went back to the ferry, loaded up three gallons of pre-mix gasoline, and brought it back to Elmo's brand new sailboat.

At this writing, Elmo's wife and daughter mentally have the sailboat up for sale in a dozen different languages and haven't been back on board since their inaugural journey.

Elmo's cellular phone bill for the three-mile ride home in his new sailboat was $432.

The little canary-yellow sailboat is now permanently tied to the dock in his secluded cove.

I think I'll wait until the middle of November when Elmo and his family are getting ready to leave for Florida for the winter, and offer to buy the sailboat from him. The time to make the deal would be when the wind is blowing 25mph and the sailboat is full of water because it's been raining two inches a day for five days in a row.

After four days of hanging onto a rope tow, your right arm would be three inches longer than your left.

POWDER SNOW

The other day, my friend Stanley called me and said,

"Hey, it just snowed two feet up on the hill and I have a foot of the stuff here in my driveway."

November 8th is a little early to think about making turns on skis, but I guess not very early when you consider the artificial snow-making machines that most resorts have today.

The first time I drove to Mammoth in my 1950 Chevy Panel delivery truck, it was a 350-mile, eight-hour drive, on a two-lane road from Los Angeles for skiing the week before Thanksgiving, 1950.

But the drive was worth it. There were two rope tows and a base lodge that was twelve feet square. They even had different "rest rooms" for men and women. The "rest rooms" were just holes in the snow with some semblance of a building around them and more ventilation than anyone would care to have.

I arrived in front of the Mammoth Tavern half-asleep, about three in the morning, climbed into my sleeping bag in the back of the truck, and slept until the car parked next to me started up about six A.M.

I thought they knew something about skiing at Mammoth that I didn't, so I sat up in bed (still wrapped in my down-filled, army-surplus sleeping bag), and pumped up and lit my Coleman stove, so I could melt the ice in the pot that I had filled with water just before I went to bed. It was solid ice, top to bottom, and by the time it thawed out, the inside of the truck was warm enough to melt the frost off the ceiling and I could start to get dressed while the oatmeal cooked. While it was cooking, I started driving up the road to where I would park and transfer to an army surplus weasel for the two or three mile ride to the rope tows. At the end of the road, there were already half a dozen other cars with their occupants in various stages of cooking breakfast, waxing skis, getting dressed, shaving, and, in general, thankful that it would be a blue-sky morning as soon as it turned gray in the east. The word around the end of the road was that,

"Dave McCoy has gone in on the weasel to pack the road down and warm up the rope tow engine and he should be back by 7:30 or 8:00."

Sure enough, he was back at the stated hour and he spun the army surplus weasel around, while the three or four ladies climbed in and rode into his base lodge. The rest of us hung onto ropes that trailed out behind for fifty or sixty feet.

Two miles later, we arrived at the 150-square-foot base lodge.

Dave had already unhitched his ropes from the wooden towers as he climbed up to the top of what was then 'the big hill,' climbed into the wooden shed that shielded the engine from the ravages of a Sierra winter, and had the rope tow running.

One by one, we paid our $2.50 to Dave's wife Roma and, clutching our rope tow grippers, began our first day of the season, skiing on Mammoth Mountain.

By the end of the day, if you could last that long, every muscle, tendon, and fiber in your body was stretched to the breaking point.

A lot of people claimed that after four days of hanging onto those ropes, your right arm would be three inches longer than your left. That generation of rope tow riders really are statistically an inch and a half taller than their children because of all of that stretching. A good friend that I used to ski with now wears a shirt with a sixteen-inch neck and 43-inch arms.

Those were the good old days at Mammoth. Today you can board an airplane at the Burbank Airport and be at Mammoth in about an hour, grab a cab to the Mammoth Mountain Inn, and find yourself a hundred yards from 31 chairlifts and a pair of Gondolas.

The only thing that is the same is Dave and Roma McCoy still own and operate the resort and the ski season that still begins in early October and ends on the Fourth of July.

Yes, they are already running several chair lifts and the early season count of lift riders reads like this: snowboarders outnumber skiers by about three to one.

In those early years, there were no big consumer ski shows, no 300-page ski magazines that start being delivered to your home in August, and no pre-season hype except for an emerging group of cinematic hobbyist.

John Jay and half a dozen other ski filmmakers were making the rounds of the major cities, showing films of far off ski resorts. Stowe, Davos, Zermatt, Magee Creek, The Sugar Bowl, places like that.

Yes, there were already at least eight or ten ski film makers in 1950, who came around with a seventy-eight rpm record player or a tape recorder, and some scratched original color film of people making turns and narrated over a microphone and got their audiences excited.

John Jay, Dick Durrance, Hans Thorner, Sverre Engen, Dr. Frank Howard, and Victor Cody, to mention a few of those early feature ski film makers. I watched all of their shows as they came through Los Angeles. None of them knew that I already had produced my very first 16mm ski film the winter before when I taught skiing in Squaw Valley.

Things were different when I produced that film. Squaw Valley had one chairlift and two rope tows, There were only three chairlifts in the state of California. But the pure feeling of a well-executed turn on the side of a hill will never change.

My first film was 16mm wide and almost an hour and a half long and I produced it with my ski instructor wages of $125 a month. The total cost was almost $500. Our latest ski film is the same width and length and cost almost a million dollars.

Things change. I recorded the musical score for my first movie in a church. I ran the ski movie on a noisy 16mm projector and a friend of mine played the church organ at 4:30 in the morning to match what she imagined the film felt like. (That was the only time we could get to use the church organ.) I made the first recording on a wire recorder and I had a lot of trouble soldering the wire where I wanted to edit a song. Every time a soldered splice went through the machine, it really made a loud bang over the PA system.

Fortunately, just before my first commercial show, my grandmother loaned me a tape recorder that she had. I transferred my wire recordings to the tape by watching the wire splices as they approached the recording head and turned the volume down on the wire recorder while the soldered splice banged through the machine.

Forty-five years ago, ski audiences had nothing to compare a musical score for a ski film to, so I managed to get away with my organ-recital, musical background for my first ski movie.

Today, the musical score is recorded, digitized, and filtered through a bunch of stuff that I know nothing about and finally comes out through the speakers in the theater sounding like it is being played live. I'm the first to admit, however, that some of the music for the movie sounds like a sack of cats on the way to the river. But then the snowboarders who are on the screen at the time also look like a sack of cats in the clothes they wear!

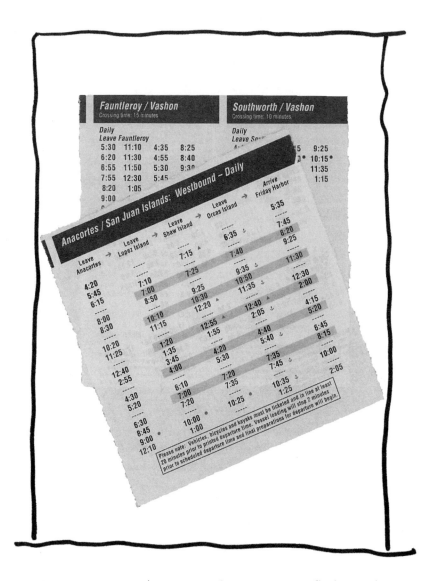

The state spent $75,000.00 for a survey to find out why their ferries were late. They discovered that they always left late, so they just printed new schedules.

THE FERRY SCHEDULE

I live on a small island up near the Canadian border that is connected to the mainland by an umbilical cord called The Ferryboat. It is owned by the state of Washington and run by a group of nameless, faceless people that almost everyone in this part of the world has bad things to say about. The waiting lines get longer each year to get on ferries that break down more and more often. We were discussing some of these problems yesterday, as I sat in a nice warm cafeteria on the top deck of a giant pile of metal that was fabricated sometime before Hitler was bombing England. I was listening to all of the people complaining, "The ferry we were on yesterday was supposed to have left at three o'clock and didn't leave until four-forty."

It was raining hard, with thirty mile per hour wind gusts, when someone at the table brought up the same old question,

"Why can't we just get a reservation on a ferry so we don't have to get to the ferry two hours early in order to get a place in line for our cars before the ferry leaves?"

"Yeah, I can get a reservation on three different airlines to get from Seattle to Greece eleven months from now. Why can't I get a reservation on the ferry tomorrow?"

I have a different attitude about this. One of the real charms of living happily on an island is putting up with some of the inconveniences.

A case in point:

My reason for going to the mainland yesterday was to pick up my car that was only about fifteen minutes from where I would get off the ferry. That's all.

To do this, I first had to find someone on the mainland who would drive me to the automobile agency that was fixing my car, then make sure my wife was available to drive me to the ferry landing in our small boat. It was raining hard when I discovered that the windshield wiper had stopped working on our small boat. Visibility was zero, so I got to drive and had to open the window and peer into the pouring rain while I steered around all the logs that float off the beaches at the spring high tides. When we finally got to the ferry landing, I was sopping wet and discovered that the ferry was a half-hour late. (You don't have to wait in line when you walk on the ferry. You only have to wait when you drive a car.)

Three years ago, the Ferry commission paid $75,000 for consultants to find out why the ferries were so often late.

The result of the study discovered the source of the problem.

The ferries all started late.

The consultant had a simple solution.

Print new schedules.

Yesterday's ferry ride was uneventful and the trip to the automobile agency didn't take too long. I had left on the ferry that was supposed to leave at ten-thirty, which left at eleven and arrived at twelve-thirty. This let me complete the car pickup by one-fifteen.

By now, I had traveled almost thirty-five miles to the agency, but felt that I had enough time to have a leisurely lunch before getting in the ferryboat line by three o'clock for the five-twenty ferryboat ride. At lunch I was told that the weekend before, the ferry-boat line was so long by eight o'clock in the morning that even with eight or ten sailings a day, they had to wait until Sunday to get on a ferry to get back home.

With that kind of information I thought, "It's Wednesday and shouldn't be a problem. I got in line at three-thirty for the five-twenty, only to be told, "You're on overload for the three o'clock ferry and the five-twenty has been canceled because the cafeteria on that ferry ran out of food. The next ferry you can get on won't be leaving until sixty-thirty."
"Maybe."

"However, you are number seventeen on overload and, with luck, you might make the three o'clock because it won't be leaving until five-fifteen."

Are you following all of this? I barely missed getting on the three o'clock ferry that left at five-fifteen.

Then I had to sit in line for the five-twenty that was cancelled and finally got on the six-thirty that left at seven forty-five. I landed on my island exactly twelve hours after I left to pick up my car.

A routine chore where, if I lived in the city, it would only have taken a half-hour at the most to complete the entire trip.

Which is probably one of the many reasons why there is so much vacant land and homes for sale on our island.

"In 1954, Courcheval, France was a brand new resort that wasn't even on a Michelin road map. When I arrived to film Emile Allais that year, there was only one gondola, a few surface lifts, and beds for less than a thousand people. Today, the Three Valleys have over two hundred lifts and accommodations for 200,000 skiers."

THE FRENCH CONNECTION

In 1949, I went to work for Emile Allais in Squaw Valley, California, as a ski instructor. At that time, Squaw Valley had one chairlift, two rope tows, and four ski instructors and, on a good day, we'd all have a pupil. I produced my first ski movie that winter, while working for $125 a month. Six years later, I was filming Emile Allais at a new ski resort once again. This one was in Courchevel, France. Today, it is part of The Three Valleys, Trois Valle, which have 214 lifts and sleep over 200,000 skiers. At that time, Courchevel had one gondola and several surface lifts and the same powder snow that the Sierras of California boasted.

The resort was so new that it was not even on the Michelin road map yet. After a long drive from Zurs, Austria, I arrived about two in the morning at the end of a dirt road and found a smoke-filled bar that was still open. With almost no knowledge of the French language, I somehow managed to get the owner to let me sleep in a corner booth after they closed up.

A few hours later, I went in search of my old friend and three times world-ski champion, Emile Allais. He was in charge of designing the resort, the ski runs, the locations of lifts - in short, the local hero. Once again, we skied and filmed together in powder snow while he told me of his plans for the future. They included an entire village that would have only ski-in, ski-out accommodations and an airport over on that ridge so skiers could fly here non-stop from

Paris, land, be met by their hotel porter and handed a ski lift ticket, so they could then ski downhill from the airport to the lift while their hotel porter took their baggage to their room. All of this would be reality before anyone thought possible.

It came about with a very simple idea.

Several former French ski champions who flew a lot of missions over the Alps during World War II made notes of every potential ski area so that when the war ended they would have a project.

Once the war was over, they convinced the French Government that there was a future in winter tourism and got the government to build roads to these high mountain locations. The government also made land available for development and the rush was on. If you built a certain number of beds in a given time frame, then you could have the land free. The money you saved in not having to pay for the land enabled you to build that many more hotel rooms. This was not unlike what the American government did for the railroads in the nineteenth century when they opened up the west.

The concept has worked simply and dramatically. A very substantial amount of taxes have been generated and thousands of jobs have been created. Until then, there was nothing there except high mountain meadows above timberline, meadows good for grazing livestock for only three or four months a year.

But I get ahead of myself.

In 1956, two days after I arrived, I had an appointment to meet Emile Allais and four ski patrolmen at the gondola building at 8:00 am. I was excited driving down to the gondola from my chalet, halfway up the mountain on one of those mornings, that you only see in a ski movie. Fourteen inches of new powder snow, crystal-clear, cobalt blue sky, and there would be no one else in the first gondola except Emile, the four ski patrolmen, and me, raring to go. I didn't notice that it had rained during the night before it turned to snow and that I was driving on black, glass ice until I did a 12 mph, 225 yard, triple 360 spin around. None of the normal automobile control devices were of any use - not the steering wheel, the throttle, the brakes, the clutch, or the glowing, plastic statue of Jesus that was mounted on the dashboard.

As I spun rather gracefully down the road without slowing down, I realized that I was rapidly approaching the back of a dump truck. I finally got a little control of the car as it slowed down to about four miles an hour and slowly slid under the back of the dump truck. Fortunately, I only did about $600 worth of damage to my $1,000 used Volkswagen bug. I also did about fifty cents worth of damage to the dump truck. Once the noise of the crash and the tinkling of glass quit echoing back and forth across the valley in the still morning air, I scrambled out of the car and, as I did, my feet slid out from under me on the black ice. Clutching the car, I staggered to my feet and inched my way towards the truck to meet the truck driver who was doing the same thing, but had something more substantial to hold onto.

I was already late to meet Emile and my skiers, so I gave him my business card, the name of the chalet where I was staying, showed him my movie equipment, a hundred French francs, (the old ones that were now worth ten new ones, or about a dollar) used Emile's name as a reference, and got him to drive out of my way so I could go on down to the gondola.

Down at the small village, I slid the car sideways, deep inside of a new snow bank, grabbed my

233

gear, raced up the steps to the gondola, met the group ten minutes later, when we got out at the top, Emile, with a twinkle in his eye said,

"Warren, I have something special, that should make a good movie for you."

With that, he pulled five red meteorological balloons out of his parka and we walked over to what looked like a tank of welding oxygen. It was a tank of helium. Emile started filling up the red balloons until they were about three or four feet in diameter and each one floating about ten feet over the heads of the ski patrolmen while tied to them with a stout string.

Emile then went on to say,

"We'll be skiing on some very steep slopes for your camera, and if any of us get caught in an avalanche we can see their balloon, follow the string down to the snow, and easily locate their bodies before they die."

Sounded like a fantastic sequence for my camera, as well as a pretty good idea for the skiers.

We figured out where everyone would ski and I set off in a long traverse with my tripod and rucksack to get set up for the first shot that was truly a sight to see. Five skiers chasing each other down a near-vertical slope while they were all being chased by giant red balloons and an avalanche that was going at the same rate of speed.

When they came to a stop on a small ridge and the avalanche went on down on both sides of them, I hollered instructions of where to go for the next shot. Then, as I started traversing across an even steeper slope, it suddenly dawned on me that I didn't have a balloon so they could find me. I was without a French Connection!

THE WATER WITCH

I married a genuine water witch.

When we were first remodeling the three-car garage on our island property into our small dream house, we had no water at all. Every evening, we drove down to the marina for our showers. Since the showers only cost a dollar each, I wanted to keep doing that and not even bother building a bathroom. But my wife wouldn't hear of it.

So we activated an old cistern on the property that had been dug in 1934. It provided enough water for an occasional shower, a lot of cooking, and the growth of a flower or two for my wife's garden.

It soon became apparent that we wouldn't have enough water for the many flowers my wife kept planting. Fortunately, it rains a lot on our island so, with a little research and a lot of money, we installed two 10,000-gallon cisterns to collect and store rain water. Then we added an ozone generator to purify it. A cubic foot of water is eight and two-thirds gallons; consequently, a square foot of roof and twenty-four inches of rain every winter will theoretically collect about seventeen gallons. We have about a thousand square feet of roof, so we collect about 17,000 gallons of water every year.

However, every spring Laurie plants more flowers, so we soon ran out of water in our cisterns. Fortunately, we discovered that we could buy 4,000 gallons of water and have it delivered for $150. Now there was no limit to the amount of flowers and vegetables she could plant. So she kept on planting them.

We also installed a gray water system so any water from the sinks, dishwasher, washing machine, and shower could be re-used to water the ever-expanding flower and vegetable garden.

Recently, the planting flowers vs. water collection battle reached the point of diminishing returns.

So, the local *reverse-osmosis-machine-salesman* entered the picture. This machine is a very complex assortment of filters, motors, pumps, and pipes that converts salt water to fresh water. With a lot of resistance from me and a lot of information from him, Laurie was irreversibly convinced that we could no longer live without a machine that will make two gallons of water a minute for her garden. Which it does! However, it is so noisy that I have spent the last five days building a soundproof building around it. Lumber to build the shed only cost $1,000 (and it doesn't even have picture windows). Now the water-making machine not only provides enough water for Laurie's garden, it also produces enough to water the grass and make it grow so I now have to mow it every five days. So far, our water-making machine has cost about the same as a Japanese pickup truck with a lot of options.

Last summer, we managed to get about thirty pounds of tomatoes, numerous lettuce salads, two six-packs of artichokes, and enough carrots to turn your eyeballs yellow, out of Laurie's garden.

I haven't done the arithmetic on the cost-per-pound of the vegetables when everything is factored in, but each pound costs approximately the same as dinner for two in a four-star restaurant.

Now that we have an ample supply of water, my wife has decided that farm-fresh eggs are the diet staples of the future. In the old foundation for the house that burned down in 1954, she had built into her garden the Taj Mahal of chicken condos. It houses a goose and nineteen chickens.

Now we have much more money invested in our water system than the three-car garage originally cost to remodel. However, the flowers are really beautiful and when we have a dinner party, the house looks like a floral shop.

Now that we have sufficient water on our property, Laurie is lobbying for a lap pool. She is a good swimmer, but in all the years I have been married to her, I have watched her swim only 112 yards. She keeps telling me it is good exercise as we enter our dotage. Jogging is also good exercise and you can do that for the cost of a pair of running shoes. A lot less than the cost of a lap pool or a reverse osmosis, water-making machine.

The deer really like to eat the flowers and the deer are winning, so now I need to buy and install about 1,000 feet of deer fence to go most of the way around our property, which is about how big Laurie's garden has become. Once I get my loan approved by the bank, I'll start building it. An automatic gate in the driveway is in the plans too. I wonder how much that will cost me, just so she won't have to get out of the car every time she drives anywhere.

By the time I pay for everything, I won't be able to afford to buy the gas to drive anywhere. In the meantime, the showers at the marina have gone up to a dollar and a half.

"The Orcas are coming."

SWIMMING WITH THE WHALES

I was hard at work yesterday, taking my mid-morning nap, when the phone rang.

It was my neighbor Elmo who said, "The Orcas are coming."

My wife Laurie, our houseguest Marilyn, and I, with my camera, piled into our 1977 powerboat and set out to get a good photo of the whales, with our house in the background as they passed by.

By the time the pod of Orcas approached the channel in front of our house, there were 37 different boats watching them. Nineteen of them were tour boats with from ten to a hundred gawking tourists aboard, most of them with a video camera. Each one had paid $50 or more to spend a couple of hours watching the Orcas come up for air every few minutes.

Last year when I followed the whales this same way, I spent so much time doing it that I finally had to get away because I developed such an uncontrollable urge to dive in and swim with them.

As I jockeyed my small boat for a good photo position, a 95-foot, fifteen-foot high cruise boat with 71 video camera operators on board came between our small boat and my house so I didn't get the picture I wanted. As I silently swore at the tour boat operator, I thought back to my first experience with Orcas.

In 1965, I got a phone call from my friend Jim Griffin in Seattle, who told me, "My brother Ted has just captured an Orca up in British Columbia. He's going to build a steel cage around it and tow the cage with the whale down to the pier alongside of Ivar's Fish House. Would you be interested in flying up and filming the whole operation?"

I struck a deal with him to supply the cameraman and film; he would pay for half of the airplane ticket and the cameraman's expenses, and I would pay the other half. We would own the footage together.

On the way to the airport, I told my photographer, Don Brolin, not to take any chances just because I had bought him a one-way ticket to Seattle.

Here is his story.

How do you film a captured whale while they are welding a steel cage around him? It was raining most of the time, the whale was black, the water was almost black, and there wasn't a whole lot to see. Welding the various sections of the cage together only took a few days and then the slow journey began. There was nothing to take movies of, but a few fifty-gallon drums being towed slowly through the water with a whale occasionally spouting in between them.

To keep his prize alive, Ted Griffin was buying salmon from any fishing boat that happened by. Over the next couple of days, Ted developed a pattern of feeding so that they could kind of figure out where Namu, the Orca was going to swim and how long it would take to get there.

The whole contraption - fifty-gallon drums, welded, steel rebar cage, towline to the tug, and the tug itself - was making about two or three mph through the darkness of the Canadian waters. Everyone on board was hoping that the wind wouldn't start blowing and break up the cage.

When Don decided that he wasn't getting any of the pictures that could pay for the expenses of the trip, he finally got into his scuba gear and slid into this moving mass of stuff. He first hung onto the outside of the cage without the camera to see how the Orca now named Namu would look.

The visibility was between five and ten feet at the most, so he had no alternative except to get inside the cage.

This was many years ago when Orcas were still thought of as killer whales that ate people for lunch. To the best of my knowledge, no one had ever been swimming with them before.

Don eased himself cautiously down inside the steel rebar cage. When he was about fifteen feet down, a dead salmon floated down in front of him. As it passed by, so did Namu and, as Don described it, Namu looked like a big black Greyhound Bus with an opening in the front as big as a eight-passenger hot tub.
That twenty-pound salmon just disappeared.

Don tried to squeeze out through the holes in the steel cage, but couldn't fit. Rather than move and attract the Orca's attention, he just hung on, holding his breath, as it again swam back the other way. Thirty seconds or so later, it swam back by and, as it did, it looked Don right in the eye.

Namu didn't even bother to slow down so, three laps, later Don went back to the surface and called for his waterproof camera.

The pictures turned out pretty much as he described them. The Orca looked like a black Greyhound Bus driving down a dark narrow alley, with an open front end that looked about as big as an eight-passenger hot tub.

We eventually sold the footage to a TV show and the Orca died a couple of years later.

Yesterday afternoon, as I sat silently in my boat with the engine off and watched seventeen

Orcas swim by, I again wanted to dive in and swim along with them. Ecological awareness has to start somewhere and maybe Namu, the first-ever captured Orca, might have been the starting point for the respect people now have for this magnificent, air-breathing mammal.

"The Orca's are here."

ASK BEFORE YOU LOWER THE BAR

Last night we had seven inches of goofer-feather powder snow fall on the mountain behind our house. This morning when I got to the ski lift, fifteen minutes before it opened, the waiting line was already about eleven snowboards long.

I was very excited because this was going to be my first day of powder snow skiing this winter. And it was already the third of April! I had missed most of the season due to shoulder surgery, followed by ten weeks of flu and bronchitis. I think I inhaled some chemical warfare germs from Saddam Hussein. My theory is that some of his government agents sprayed a rare mutated flu and bronchitis germ in a passenger plane when it stopped near Iraq. That same plane flew on to New York, where one of the passengers transferred to a direct flight to Colorado to go skiing. The next morning that passenger was sitting next to me on a chairlift and gave me some of those Saddam Hussein flu germs and there went my winter.

But back to riding the lift for first tracks in goofer-feather powder snow at the beginning of April. I managed three quick runs in some of my secret places before IT happened.

The lower terminal of the lift, which had been in the warm spring sun for a week, followed by four days of rain, had created a lake around tower #1. Last night's cold had formed a thin layer of ice over this lake, which was now snow-covered.

I had just sat down on the chairlift and was bending over to loosen the buckles on my left boot when the foot and armrest bar hit me in the back of the head. Some over-eager skier riding in the chair with me had lowered it without asking the rest of us on the chair if we were ready. The bar hit me hard enough to knock me right off the chair. Fortunately, I was only about four feet in the air, so I crash-landed and began coasting down into what was a lake yesterday and an ice and powder snow-covered lake today. I knew I could easily coast across it and walk back to get a later chair.

I managed to coast halfway across what had been a two-foot deep pond before ice broke.

Instantly, I was standing in knee-deep water on this beautiful, sunny, powder-snow morning. I quickly discovered that it is very hard to lift a ski out from under the ice while trying to get up on top of it without breaking off more ice.

Exhausted within thirty seconds, I figured out that I would have to reach down into the icy cold water and take my skis off. By then, I had broken a hole in the ice about ten feet in diameter.

My powder snowsuit was wet up to its knees, my ski boots were full of water, and now my right sleeve was wet up to my shoulder. I did have the presence of mind to throw my poles and gloves far enough away so that I might be able to retrieve them once I got back out in the powder snow, instead of under the thin ice.

While I was wallowing in this frozen hell, people were gliding overhead on the quad chairlift at the rate of 2,500 an hour. They were all going to get to track up that powder snow that was supposed to be mine. And every one of them had some remark to make about how dumb I was.

It seemed like an eternity before one of the lift operators finally quit loading passengers and came over to help me.

I asked him to throw me a shovel or something that I could use to break the thin ice and make my way out to shallower water more easily. It took about ten minutes to break my way through the ice before I was back high, but not dry, on powder snow-covered ground.

By my calculations, in the ten minutes I spent trying to get out of that frigid snow and ice-covered water, 417 skiers and snowboarders had ridden right over my head on the quad chairlift. Not one of them offered any advice that could have helped me.

Once out of the pond, I had two alternatives: Stay most of the day in the lift shack while I waited for my clothes and boots to dry out, or
Ride up on the chairlift to a trail that would let me ski back down to my house. (The ride up would take six minutes, and skiing down would take four or five. Could I get back to my house before my water-soaked equipment would begin to freeze solid? Once it froze, would I still be able to execute a turn with my powder snowsuit frozen solid? Would the fabric break if it froze while I was still wearing it?)

I staggered into the lift shack to phone my wife to get her to bring up some dry clothes and boots for me.

I got our answering machine.

The heater in the lift shack was so worn out that it would have taken eleven years to boil a cup of water. My decision was made! It was sunny, it was only twenty degrees, it was 10am, and my skiing in untracked powder snow was finished for the day.

I decided to get on the lift - no footrest this time. While riding up, I didn't even try to explain what had happened to me to the three other people who were on the lift with me.

Before I started skiing down, I had to scrape the icicles off the bottoms of my skis so I didn't have to walk down. Once that was done, I know I set a new record from the top of the mountain to the front door of my house.

No, frozen fabric doesn't break if you ski fast.

But, please ask before you lower the bar!

HUMPIE HUNTING

Every other year, pink salmon, called hump-ies, come cruising through the archipelago where I live. As many as twenty million of them swim by an island near our home and head up the Fraser River in Canada. They always do it during the week before and the week after Labor Day. The trick, of course, is to try to catch your daily limit of four so you can have fresh, smoked, frozen, or pickled salmon all winter long.

Humpies travel in schools on or near the sur-face, so the dorsal fin can be easily spotted. When you see one or more of them, you jam the throttle of your boat forward and race over to where you saw them. Coasting to a stop, you grab your spinning rod and cast a lure called a Buzz Bomb out in front of the school. If you do it right, you can hook one almost every time you cast.

I have a small, outboard motor on the inflat-able dinghy on the bow of our big boat that we take to Alaska. Just before I left for humpie hunting, I decided to take the outboard off the dinghy and move it over to our 20-foot fishing boat just in case I had any problems. Since it weighs almost a hundred pounds, it is not easy to wrestle off the dinghy and carry along the narrow deck of the big boat to the dock and finally onto my small boat. Once there, I have to wrestle it into the forward cabin where I store it in anticipation of one of my inevitable disasters.

About an hour later, with Dwain Colby, I met Bruce Barr at Roche Harbor where we flipped a coin to see which boat we would take. He lost, so we went out in his boat. We headed out to where there were 75 or 80 other boats humpie hunting. But not like Bruce does it. He can see a one-inch dorsal fin break the water as far as three-quarters-of-a-mile away. Before a couple of hours were up, all four of us on his boat had our limits.

We had to quit fishing early because my wife, Laurie, was giving her father an 80th birthday party. At 5:30pm, I remembered I should have been at the party about twelve miles away at 4:30pm.

I took my share of the salmon to my boat and loaded them aboard while Dwain untied the boat, and then we headed home. From Roche Harbor, there is a five-knot speed limit for the first mile. Once we got past the last speed buoy, I began cruising at 27 knots until, about two miles later, the engine coughed and died.

I had run out of gas.

When this happens, I get to wrestle my hundred-pound outboard motor out of the forward compartment, stagger to the back of the boat with it, and then try to hang it on a small piece of plywood called a motor mount. I always tie a rope around a motor when I do this so it won't sink clear to the bottom when I drop it.

To sit on the edge of a rocking-and-rolling, small boat with a hundred-pound motor in your lap and eventually wrestle it over the transom while you try to line up the mount on the motor with the mount on the boat and get it right the first time, is not an easy trick. It is such a dumb thing to have to do, I can't compare it to anything else you or I might be familiar with. It is just plain dumb to run out of gas.

Meantime, the party-time clock was ticking

Your date waited for you at chair #11 at ten and you waited for her at chair #10 at eleven.

When the ski lift operators finally let you on the lift at 8:30am with fourteen inches of new powder snow, the new snow is already tracked up by thirty-seven ski instructors who have been riding the lift since 7:30. They complain, because they have only had five runs each before the paying customers get to ride.

The buckles on your ski boots only break when you are tightening them up to get ready to make first tracks.

Why is it that we are all so determined to ski when there are so many things working against us – mainly our bodies?

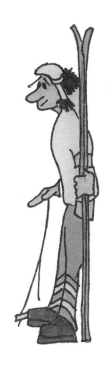

"When?"

RETIREMENT

The other day the phone rang and it was my old friend, Mort Klusudnik.

"Hi Warren. Your name came up at lunch today and we wanted to know what you are doing with all of your time now that you're retired and living on that island?"

This set me to wondering about what I DO do. So today I kept a log of what it is like to sit around on an island all day, enjoying retirement.

Four nights ago the raccoons killed my wife's pet goose, so yesterday I went to the lumber yard and bought a raccoon trap, while my wife stopped at the pet store to buy a rabbit to replace the goose.

This morning there was a big fat raccoon in the trap, so I had to carry the trap down to my small, inflatable boat and then motor over to a nearby island and let it go where it could bother someone else's livestock.

As I was loading up the trap with the raccoon in it, my friend Marvin from across the pass motored up to the dock and climbed out of his boat with a raccoon in a trap just like mine. He told me he always dumped the raccoons he caught over here on the island where we live.

"Damn things keep killing my wife's chickens."

When I got back from completing my mission of raccoon migration, I had to put the tools away from a weekend of working on my wife's "*HONEY DO*" list.

The shovel and hoe went into the garden storage shed. The wheelbarrow and the two extra bags of cement went to the garage along with the trowel, level, wire brush, hammer, nails, rake, broom, three plastic buckets, assorted pieces of wood, and the remains of a roll of thirty-pound felt. The garage is two hundred feet from the rock wall I built for her and about thirty feet higher up the side of a hill behind the house.

After I got the tools put away, I sent a fax to a publisher to O.K. the cover for my 1999, colored, ski-action calendar.

Last week the engine on my boat quit, so I have had to cruise around in my small inflatable dinghy. It's only ten feet long and about as flexible as a waterbed with an engine. I had to sit in the back of it so I can steer the outboard motor and that makes it ride like it is sinking at the stern. So, I found a piece of PVC pipe and a couple of hose clamps in my garage somewhere and made an extension handle for the engine.

Now I can sit anywhere I want to in the boat and it rides a lot better. Wherever I sit though, it still folds up a little bit.

I haven't been able to close the side door to my garage ever since I finished building it this spring, so I planed and sanded the door down so it would close before the heavy rainy season really gets here. Now I have to schedule a trip to the lumber yard some day to buy a doorknob for it.

During lunch, I made some rough sketches for a cartoon birthday card for my friend's seventieth birthday party.

The tide was now about right, so I loaded up my crab pots and started to drive the two miles to where I think the crabs are living today. Before I did that, I had to pump up all of the chambers in the inflatable because the day was overcast, the water was cold, and the air inside had contracted and made the boat really sag wherever I touched it. The trip to the crab area was uneventful except for the seven-knot tide that roared through the pass at full flood. My inflatable will go fifteen knots, so it is no big deal. Once there, I baited the pots with frozen salmon heads and tails and put them over the side.

When I got back home, there was a phone call from my publisher about delivery of the galley proofs for my new book. We had to coordinate which island the floatplane would deliver the proofs to on Thursday. It all depends on which island they have to deliver a paying passenger to, so I can meet the plane at that island. Then I had to check on the ferry schedule in case it was too foggy to fly my book up here or the paying passenger canceled and the flight didn't happen.

About that time, Laurie's new rabbit got out. The rabbit doesn't live in the cage because her goose was killed in it. We have an old, burned-out basement foundation on our property that my wife keeps turning into an ever-enlarging garden. It is sur- rounded by another, larger garden and a six-foot- high deer fence. The rabbit got out of the basement foundation garden, into the outer garden and out of that garden through a hole in the deer fence that I was going to fix last month.

I had to climb up to the garage, get my salmon net, and help her chase the rabbit for about twenty minutes. Between Laurie, our dog Pepper, and my salmon net, we finally managed to corner it between the dock and a rock and return it to the basement foundation where the cage is in which the raccoon killed her goose.

The wind started blowing, so I had to zip up the flaps on our guest tent to keep all of the Madrona leaves and fir tree needles from blowing into the bed so our next guests won't have too much to complain about.

The wind was about seven or eight knots by now and so I hustled back out to get my crabs out of the pots. The first pot I pulled up had a can of Miller beer in it and an anonymous note from someone thanking me for the six crabs.

Fortunately, the next three pots delivered six keepers.

Time for an afternoon snack. If I lean against the bulletin board on the refrigerator just right, I can erase some of the things on Laurie's *HONEY DO* list. I did.

I took another quick look through the galleys for the book and decided to change two of the illustrations. While I was working on the drawings, the phone rang and I accepted an invitation to speak at Keystone, Colorado, next January; then Laurie told me she had accepted a book-signing appearance for me in Burlington, Vermont in late November.

Since the crab pots still had some bait left in them, I had left them out, so I had to make another trip to retrieve them and got caught by darkness. Before I left, Laurie made me wear my new float coat that glows in the dark in case I fall overboard. I retrieved a half dozen more crabs and had to clean them on the dock in the dark.

After dinner, I was standing in the shower thinking how boring it is to be retired, and, once again, spend an entire day without getting in a car to go somewhere to do something.

Ah, retirement. What bliss!

WHERE DO WE GO FROM HERE?

I'm busy working on next year's feature-length ski film and, as I approach my fiftieth anniversary of film-making in 1999, I have been looking back through some of the hundreds of thousands of feet of film I have been involved with creating during the last forty-nine years. It is surprising to me how many of the skiers I knew so well are no longer alive.

Some of them have met death riding in a hang glider, or a bicycle in heavy traffic, others in ski crashes, avalanches, or old age. By this time in my life, my list has grown very long. The reasons that my friends are no longer around are as many and as varied as my friends who aren't.

What is surprising is some of the ways they have chosen to be remembered after they are gone.

One of the men who skied in our films engraved names on tombstones for a living; however, he worked in an area of Canada where the ground is frozen for almost six months out of the year. The gravedigger couldn't dig graves then, so he always had the winter off to ski. His business card said, "Marble engraver. Eventually yours." Which I think says it all. Especially since he already has engraved his own tombstone. Except he hasn't filled in the final date yet. Someone else will have to do that for him.

One of my sailing friends always said that when he died he wanted to be buried at sea and come back as a seal. For his funeral, all of us went out in our various small boats and floated around while we listened to the preacher deliver his sermon. After that, his son held the carton containing his ashes out over the side of the boat and stuck a knife into the bottom of it so the ashes would flow out. Within a minute or so of when the ashes landed in the water, a seal came up in the center of our ring of boats and barked loudly at us, as if to say, "I got my wish."

Everyone who saw that seal, has never forgotten him, because we all know that we saw a smile on its face.

But, getting back to some of my skiing friends and how they wanted to be remembered.

A good friend who is getting along in years and was a real pioneer in the ski industry by developing a ski resort told me recently at dinner,

"When it's my time to go, I want to get cremated and put in the snow-making machinery and get shot out onto the slope in the form of snowflakes."

Yesterday, while I was riding the ferryboat to the mainland, the same subject of death came up and a retired local person told this story.

He said that he and half a dozen of his friends had skied together most of their lives. "You know, the old gang gets together every year for a week or two and goes somewhere. Just the guys, no wives!

Well, old Charlie died last winter, and when his will was read, it sounded like a good idea to us."

The will read:

"I want to be cremated and then I want you to mix my ashes with the best ski wax you can figure out for that day. Put it on the bottom of your skis and spend the day skiing all over our favorite runs at our favorite resort, thinking of me while you're doing it. That way, I know I will be where I want to be forever. All over some of best ski slopes in the world."

This sounded like a good idea, but his five friends discovered that no matter how they tried to mix ashes with ski wax, it didn't slide very well.

They all did what he had asked of them, skiing all day with the worst wax in the history of skiing. It took almost a black diamond run before they could even go fast enough to make a turn.

That wax and ashes are still there today, except where the spring runoff took it on down into the creek.

Which brings up an interesting point.

Scientists say that since the world began, no new water has ever been created. Water just evaporates from the ocean and eventually falls back to earth in the form of rain or snow. With that in mind, there is a mathematical chance that those snowflakes that covered your goggles the last time you had a good powder snow day could have fallen on Napoleon's shoulders during the battle of Waterloo or maybe onto Genghis Khan's shoulders as he rode into Manchuria. The water that snowflakes are made of that you are shoveling today could have fallen as a raindrop on the back of one of the two elephants as they were marching onto Noah's ark.

What goes around definitely comes around when you are talking about water.

Someone said, "Nothing lasts forever." However, I think that whatever snowflakes are made of does last forever!

*"I don't think anyone should ever
forget where they got started."*

Alta, Utah 1946

WARREN MILLER

for sale
... from his
Private Collection

©W.MILLER

The originals of these bronzes were carved in walnut in approximately 1900. Warren discovered them in Kleinescheidig, Switzerland, in 1953. Much admired as a part of his film company's office decoration for many years, he created a limited edition of fifty sets in bronze. The man is twenty-one inches tall, the lady sixteen. Their elegant, soft patinas make them a lovely addition to your office or home.

For further information contact
Laurie Miller at P.O. Box 350,
Deer Harbor, WA 98243
fax 360-376-6489
or e-mail wmiller@thesanjuans.com

LITHOGRAPHS OF WARREN'S ORIGINAL DRAWINGS

These pen and ink drawings were made after the Harriman Cup in Sun Valley, Idaho, in 1948. Warren drew the originals on a dining room table in the Challenger Inn when he was living in the nearby parking lot. They have been lithographed in a limited edition of five hundred and each one is hand painted, numbered, and signed by Warren.

Any one of these lithographs, or the set of five, will make a great gift for the people who have loaned you their condominium for your annual ski vacation; or hang them in your office so you can be reminded of why you work so hard.
Each lithograph can be individually autographed by Warren to the purchaser or anyone they designate.

WARREN MILLER
APRIL 1948

$115
HAND PAINTED
BY
WARREN MILLER

Warren Miller when he still had hair and was teaching skiing at Sun Valley, Idaho. Warren has produced over five hundred sports films during his fifty-year career of lurching from one near-disaster to the next as he wandered the world with his camera. He refuses to retire. $400.00

Jack Reddish, from Salt Lake City, was on the 1948 U.S. Olympic team and, in 1950, won the National Slalom Championship by eight seconds and was seventeen seconds ahead of the third place finisher. He went on to work in Hollywood. $300.00

Barney McLean was the captain of the 1948 Olympic Ski Team in St. Moritz. He started his career as a nordic ski jumper and his experience at high speeds in the air helped him become one of America's most successful ski racers. He enjoyed a long career in the ski industry and is now retired. $300.00

Leon Goodman taught skiing at Sun Valley, Idaho, for many years, until he moved to a small town in northern Idaho where he owned and managed a bowling alley until retiring in McCall Idaho. $300.00

Toni Matt was born and raised in Austria and came to America to teach skiing for Hannes Schneider at North Conway, New Hampshire, in the mid 1930's. He achieved instant fame when he skied straight down the headwall at Tuckerman's Ravine. He spent many years skiing at North Conway. $300.00

Other books about Warren's outrageous lifestyle

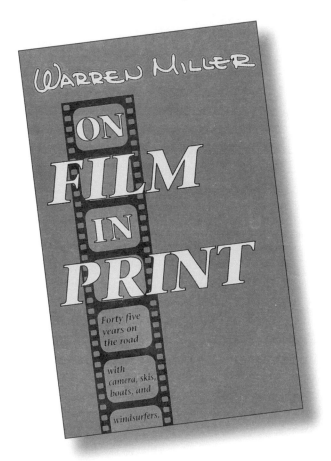

Warren has been skiing and surfing since 1937, and has spent most of the last fifty years on the road with camera and skis, boats and windsurfers, while chasing freedom, finding it, and filming it. This is his 1994 limited-edition collection of almost fifty stories about his unusual lifestyle while traveling the world from New Zealand to Zermatt, from Malibu to Maui, and a lot of other places in between.

$12.95 soft cover and $24.95 hard cover

"WINE,
WOMEN,
WARREN,
& SKIS"

WARREN MILLER

The hilarious saga of Warren's six-month ski trip during the winter of '46-'47 while living on oyster crackers and ketchup, frozen rabbits, poached ducks, goat meat, and powder snow. He slept in an eight-foot-long trailer-at-eight- below zero in the parking lots of the finest ski resorts in the west. Learn how to ski for a hundred days in Sun Valley, Idaho, for only $18 and at Alta Utah for $2.50 a week. And there are lots of antique photos to prove it.
$10.95 soft cover.
Ninety minute audio-tape of this book narrated by Warren.
$11.95.

Warren Miller's lifestyle is like no other!
For your copy of these books or cassette, send your check or Visa/MasterCard number with the expiration date to Warren Miller, P.O. Box 350 Deer Harbor, Washington 98243. Or Fax 360 376 6489 or email to wmiller@thesanjuans.com. Include additional $5.00 for shipping and handling for up to three books and an extra $3.75 for each additional copy. Allow a couple of weeks for delivery.